WHAT KNOT?

WHAT KNOT?

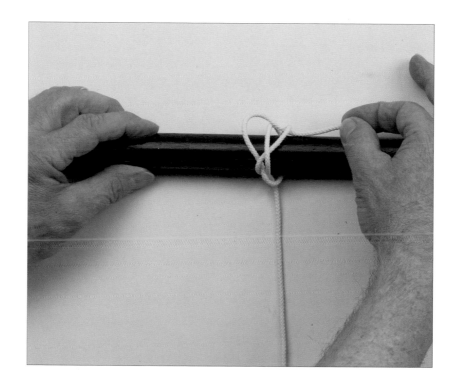

Geoffrey Budworth &
Richard Hopkins

CHARTWELL
BOOKS

This edition published in 2007 by
CHARTWELL BOOKS
an imprint of Book Sales
a division of Quarto Publishing Group USA Inc.
142 West 36th Street, 4th Floor
New York, New York 10018
USA

Reprinted in 2007, 2010, 2011, 2012,
2013, 2014, 2015, 2016

© **Regency House Publishing Limited**
The Manor House
High Street
Buntingford
Hertfordshire
SG9 9AB
United Kingdom

For all editorial enquiries please contact:-
www.regencyhousepublishing.com

ISBN-13: 978-0-7858-2223-3

Printed in China

Contents

Caution!
The contents of this book are
intended only as a general
introduction to knot-tying. Before
using any of the knots, bends,
hitches, loops, et cetera, either at
work or leisure in a possibly
hazardous situation, where there is a
perceived risk of personal injury,
death, damage to (or loss of)
property, it is advisable to consult a
qualified practitioner to ensure they
are correctly tied and suitable for
the purpose for which they are
being used.

RIGHT: Jury Mast Knot.

*OPPOSITE: Zoomorphs: an original Celtic artwork
designed by Julie Budworth.*

It's only a lump on a length of line,
A snarl in a piece of string.
But properly tied, by a practised hand,
It becomes such a beautiful thing.

It is square. It is round. It can slip or hold fast.
That depends on the job that's required.
But when it's complete, all tucked in and neat,
It is really a sight to admire.

We splice it or hitch it. Make becket or bend,
Tie a grommet, an eye or a chain,
Make a sling or a sinnet, a noose or a net,
And none of them looks quite the same.

Be it useful or fancy, for work or display,
If it's used once or twice or a lot,
There's nothing quite like it to make you feel proud,
Than knowing that you tied the knot.

The knots that I learned under canvas and pine,
At Scout camps in days long ago,
Are as handy today as they were in my youth,
But back then I just didn't know …

That those lumps on a line and those snarls in a string,
Would linger and not be forgot,
And foster a love for more knowledge and skill,
As I struggle to learn one more knot.

© David J. Shaw 2005

INTRODUCTION

Anyone can tie knots. Learn just one or two and you will be glad you bought this book. Learn ten knots, and you may well find you have an aptitude for them that could change your outlook on life. This is because there is endless pleasure to be had from studying and practising knots. Knotting is a fundamental but fascinating process, being an art, craft, science and philosophy, all rolled into one. There are thousands of knots and hundreds of books on the subject, while the International Guild of Knot Tyers is a worldwide association of people sharing a common interest in all aspects of the subject.

The ability to tie a few basic bends and bindings, hitches, loops and lashings, is an invaluable skill that separates the useful individual from the mere onlooker. As well as being able to ride a bicycle, change an electric fuse, read a map, drive a car, swim, and perform first aid in an emergency, everyone should know a few knots. It makes good sense to shed our over-dependence on buckles, clips and zip-fasteners, safety pins and superglue, when a length of cord or rope and the right choice of knot works at least as well, and often better.

THE LURE & LORE OF KNOTS

In the deep past, before humankind knew how to make fire or a wheel, to harness the wind, cultivate the soil, or even, perhaps, to string sounds into sentences, they tied knots.

The ancient Greeks enjoyed tying knots that were difficult to undo. When that megalomaniac warlord Alexander the Great encountered the 'impossible' Gordian knot, the legend tells how he slashed through it with his sword, which is why to think positively to resolve a problem is still referred to as 'cutting the Gordian knot'.

The Greek philosopher Plato (c.428–347 BCE) declared that those who preyed upon the gullible by means of knot sorcery should be put to death; and as late as 1713 the Bordeaux parliament in France sentenced a person to be burned alive for allegedly bewitching an entire family by means of magic knots.

Greek and Roman physicians used knots as surgical slings and the scientist and historian, Pliny the Elder (23–79 CE), wrote that wounds that had been bound with the *Nodus Herculanus* or Herculean knot (the modern-day reef or square knot) healed quicker. This seems to have been the first eponymous knot, named after a person, although there have been many such knots since.

The practice of surveying land in ancient Egypt required a long rope, knotted at intervals, and a functionary called a *harpendonapate* (literally a rope-stretcher) used three slaves to pull the rope taut by the knots, so as to form a

9

both skull shrines and carved stone heads and the motif of the head runs through Celtic myths, from that of Bran's sacred head, as told in the early medieval Irish epic poem, *The Voyage of Bran*, to tales of ritual beheadings elsewhere.

Celtic shamanism not only encompassed mutability, or the ability to change shape or take the form of animals (zoomorphism), it was also closely linked to the earth, animism (the attribution of a living soul to plants, inanimate objects and natural phenomena), and the cycle of life and death. It was possible to be mutated through strong emotions, or to gain special insight through a powerful experience. But what connects dreamtime mythologies throughout the world, is the mysterious concept that the boundaries that exist between mankind and the rest of the natural world, the animal world in particular, are unstable and can be crossed.

The cult of the human head, and collecting the heads of enemies to obtain their power, is an example of the continuing cycle of the spirit life. To possess someone's head amounted to possessing their soul, spirit and personal attributes, echoes of which can be found in other cultures, where the heart or brain of a noble warrior or a respected foe was eaten in order to obtain something of his strength and prowess. Thus the spirit does not die, but is transferred to the possessor of the head, when the qualities of its original owner merge with his own.

It is not known for sure if the ancient Celts attributed any particular meaning to their intricate knotwork designs and they may not have been the first to have created such forms, but may have received their influences from the Norsemen. Some ascribe arcane magical properties to the knotwork designs, but it may simply have been that the very act of creating such designs, whose very intricacy so actively engaged the conscious mind, may have had the effect of setting the unconscious free. This is not a very different technique from the repetitive recitation of a mantra, or telling one's rosary beads, and may have had similar results.

The skull illustrated, manufactured by Skullywags, is a modern collectible, and the fact that it is covered in Celtic knot motifs is of little significance other than that they are highly decorative. However, the Celts did indeed seem to have had a cult of the head, and to have worshipped it, regarding it as the abode or seat of the spirit. Archeological digs have revealed

INTRODUCTION

triangle. This meant that a rope knotted at 30, 40 and 50 yards will make a right angle between the 30- and 40-yard sides. Indeed, the Greek word for the side opposite the right angle of such a triangle, or hypotenuse, originally meant 'stretched against'.

Many illiterate peoples once used knotted cords to record and recall genealogical family trees, or as calendars and calculators, such as the abacus, which evolved from knots on strings. Knots also crop up in religion, and the current craze in South America for the Virgin Mary as 'an untyer of knots' is only one aspect of her iconography. Rosary beads were once knotted cords and the knots on the waist-ties of monks and nuns still bind them symbolically to their vows. It has even been suggested that knotted cords were used as an early form of writing.

During the days of square-rigged warships and merchant ships, dockyard riggers and seagoing mariners took ropework further than ever before. The stopper knot, known as Matthew Walker's knot (pages 242–243) seems to have been the second knot to be named after a person. He is thought to have been

RIGHT: A design for a knot garden, from L'Agriculture et Maison Rustique, by Charles Estienne, 1570, revised and augmented by J. Liebaut in 1586.

OPPOSITE: The Elizabethan Knot Garden, the Old Palace, Hatfield House, Hertfordshire, England.

Historic Hatfield House is one of the most beautiful Jacobean houses in England. The Old Palace was completed in 1496 and the building of Hatfield House was begun on a site next to the Old Palace in 1609 and completed in 1611. It was here that Elizabeth I, the daughter of Henry VIII, spent her childhood, and where she held her first Council of State in the banqueting hall in 1558. It remains the home of the Cecil family to this day. The knot garden, situated in front of the Old Palace, is based on Elizabethan designs and was created by the Dowager Marchioness of Salisbury in 1984. For authenticity, only plants known to have grown in England before 1700 were used in the design.

Renaissance gardens were similar to the one at Hatfied, and were referred to as knots by the English, as occasionally were mazes, until they came to be known as parterres in the 17th century. Knot gardens were laid out in symmetrical and intricate geometrical forms, usually contained within square compartments, each separated from the other by the garden's main pathways. During the early 16th century, as was typical of ancient Roman gardens, as well as those of the Middle Ages, compartments were enclosed by waist-high hedges or lattice fences.

A small garden may have had only a single compartment, while one that was more elaborate would have had eight or more. Hedging was of

clipped box (Buxus sempervirens), being the easiest to maintain, but herbs such as marjoram, thyme, costmary, hyssop, lemon balm and southernwood, clipped to form interlacing ribbons of colourful and aromatic vegetation, were also used. Spaces within compartments could be more solidly planted, either to produce blocks of a single colour or a pleasing combination of several. Hedges were often punctuated by large topiary features set at regular intervals.

Throughout the 16th century, each compartment was invariably given its own unique knot pattern and planting, though two compartments facing one another across a main pathway could be mirror images of each other, though this was rare. During the first part of the 17th century, cutwork parterres were de rigueur, created by the ever more intricate designs. These resulted in the smaller, segregated planting areas favoured by the Dutch, which they planted with the tulips then being introduced from Turkey. This was the start of tulipomania in Europe, when staggering prices could be paid for a single bulb.

a rigger, who was employed in the ship-building industry in north-east England in around 1750. Walker and his wife are thought to have lived on board an old converted hulk in Sunderland, moored near Folly End on the Monkwearmouth shore of the River Wear.

Some believe the childish pastime of cat's cradle came to England from the Orient by way of tea clippers, possibly between 1650 and 1720. By the late 19th and early 20th centuries, however, anthropologists had discovered that such string figures had probably always existed, on continents and oceanic archipelagos around the world, where they were used by primitive, but not necessarily simple, cultures to illustrate stories of mythological, religious and magical significance. String figures became a tool by which scholars, engaged in ethnological research, were able to clarify previously obscure tribal origins and migrations.

A few heraldic designs, representing a personal or family lineage or ancient allegiance, take the form of knots, the Wake (or Ormonde) knot and the Josephine knot both being Carrick Bends (see page 154), while the Cavendish knot is in fact a figure-of-eight (see page 70).

In medieval literature allusions are made to a 'true lover's knot', though it is unclear if such a knot really existed or was merely a romantic metaphor used by poets and playwrights. But it became quite the fashion in 16th-century Europe to plant 'knot gardens', where evergreen shrubs were used to create ribbons of intertwining geometrical patterns.

The first manuals of seamanship to illustrate knotting appeared in the late 1700s and early 1800s, while how-to

LEFT: Maria Knotenlöserin, Mary the Untyer of Knots, 1700.

This is the work of the German painter, Johann Melchior Georg Schmittdner, and the painting is currently the altarpiece of the church of St. Peter am Perlach in Augsburg. Twenty years ago, a copy of the painting found its way to South America, where it became an object of immediate veneration. The popularity of Mary as an untyer of knots, with the power to solve problems, particularly of the matrimonial variety, has currently reached its apogee in Brazil, where a church honouring her in this capacity has been erected in Buzios, near Rio de Janeiro.

OPPOSITE: Sub-dividing the sky into a geometric jigsaw puzzle, the standing and running rigging of a large square-rigged sailing ship requires multifarious ropes to harness the wind that enables it to roam the oceans of the world. These include braces, brails and bridles; bowlines and buntlines; blocks-&-falls (tackles); footropes and ratlines; shrouds and stays; sheets and halyards. Together they can amount to as much as 30 miles (48km) of assorted cordage weighing several tons.

INTRODUCTION

LEFT: All who venture afloat must quickly learn to tame and handle ropes.

OPPOSITE: Climbers too must 'know the ropes', and the life-support knots that are so aptly named.

books of instruction, such as this, were 20th-century developments. If Helen of Troy's face really did launch a thousand ships, then she was the cause of a clutch of nautical knots being invented too. But seamen can no longer be described in terms of 'every hair a rope's yarn, every finger a marlinspike', for today it is anglers and climbers who, more than anyone else, devise and name the new knots, or the modifications of ones that already exist. There are even a few aficionados of computer-assisted design, who not only draw animated knots, but also produce even more elaborate creations in 3D.

People of every continent and culture, country and climate, have ended up having more or less the same knots. Notable exceptions are the intertwined knot designs, referred to as Celtic knotting, that survive in early illuminated manuscripts, such as the Book of Kells, and in Irish and Anglo-Saxon stone

carvings, left behind by the Picts and Scots. With its characteristic rhomboid panels, key patterns, and depictions of semi-human figures known as zoomorphs, Celtic knots now adorn anything from beer mats and dress fabrics to kitchen towels.

Chinese knotting is unique, in that it combines tassels with beads and semi-precious stones, using a colour palette of breathtaking beauty to embellish objects that are already ornamental in themselves, such as palace lanterns, wind chimes, fans, hairpins, garments and spectacle cases.

Japanese knotting is also highly decorative, used in the gift-wrapping of parcels and containers, as well as in the paraphernalia used in tea ceremonies, while Kumihimo encompasses the ancient art of fine braiding.

Macramé or square-knotting is believed to have been Moorish in origin, reaching Europe via Spain, then crossing the sea from the Netherlands to England with Queen Mary, the wife of William of Orange. A later devotee was Queen Charlotte, the consort of the desperately sad but mad King George the Third. Revivals of macramé have occurred from time to time, the last in the 1970s. This regrettably took the form of how-to kits for making an owl, a pot-hanger or a shopping bag, when the craft can be used for so much more.

Since the cravat was replaced by the necktie, at least 85 ways of tying it have been identified, although only half-a-dozen or so, such as the four-in-hand and the Windsor knot, have proved lastingly popular.

Most people think of Scouting and yachting whenever knots are mentioned, and this may once have been true; nowadays, however, Scouts have other things to occupy their minds and there is little scope for knotting aboard modern boats. But there are many other individuals who have always tied and continue to tie more knots than Scouts and sailors. They include trades, callings and pursuits as distinct and disparate as anglers and archers, basket-makers, bellringers and bookbinders, builders and butchers, circus performers, climbers and cavers, conjurors or magicians and escapologists, engineers (civil and military), falconers, farmers, firemen and deep-sea fishermen, gardeners, horsemen and horsewomen, kite-flyers, poachers, prospectors and other wilderness pioneers, scuba divers, steeplejacks and surgeons, theatrical riggers, truck drivers, remedial therapists and weavers.

The rest of us tie knots because we find doing so an absorbing pastime, quite as satisfying as completing a crossword or jig-saw puzzle. For those seeking greater challenges, however, there is something more than the mere 'hippie engineering' (to quote the satirical American writer, P.J. O'Rourke, commenting on a rope walkway in a jungle treetop). There is the theory of knots, both abstract and applied, both of which are underpinned by rigorous mathematical formulae and algorithms. Proponents and practitioners of knotting are able to tie a Turk's head in the form of a Möebius band and are comfortable with the concept that knots cannot exist in four dimensions, though they can be untied this way. In 1992, the New Zealand mathematician Dr. Vaughan Jones, FRS, was awarded a Field's Medal (the mathematical equivalent of a Nobel Prize) following his discovery of a new polynomial for knots and links; he became a vice-

WHAT KNOT?

president for life of the International Guild of Knot Tyers the following year.

Since the creation of the IGKT in 1982, the evolution of knotting has taken a quantum leap. More than 100 original knot books and booklets have been produced by guild members, and new terms, tools and techniques have begun to emerge. Fresh knots continue to be discovered or devised, and a few suitably qualified individuals have been called on to assist criminal investigators and courts of justice in the forensic analysis and evaluation of knots and ligatures discovered at the scenes of crimes.

CORDAGE

Rope always seems to have been with us, in fact, long before records of its existence

actually recall. Most ancient cultures – the Egyptians, Chinese and Persians, to name but three – were accomplished ropemakers, and so later were the Venetians. Until the 20th century, however, ropemaking remained a skilled but low-tech operation, mostly done by hand in fields, open yards or long sheds, where workers walked to and fro, hour after hour, to spin the long yarns and lay them up into strands and completed ropes. A rope could only be as long as the 'ropewalk' where it was made. Nowadays the machines to manufacture synthetic cordage are compact and vertical, working more like maypole dancers, and making the ropewalk obsolete. Many towns and cities still have streets or apartment blocks named 'The Ropewalk', indicating their original purpose which has long since ceased to exist. The contribution once made by women to the trade is reflected in the English harbour town of Poole, in Dorset, in the area once occupied by the Longfleet Rope Company, which is still known as the 'Ladies' Walking Field'.

Cordage used for knotting has a few general terms of its own. If thicker than 10mm (0.4 inches), it is a rope, while anything smaller is cord, twine, string or thread. Knot tyers also refer with lazy familiarity to cordage as 'stuff' (cheap stuff, good stuff, old stuff). A rope dedicated to a particular function becomes a line (mooring line, towline, lifeline, fishing line, washing line).

Depending upon the tension built into it during manufacture, cordage may be soft-laid (floppy, flexible and just right for learning how to tie and on which to demonstrate knots), or hard-laid (tight, stiff and less easy to manipulate).

The thickness of ropes made of natural fibres used to be measured in inches, according to their circumference, making the expression 'a three-inch hawser' somewhat misleading since, in appearance, it was a little less than an inch thick. Synthetic cordage is more realistically measured according to its diameter in millimetres. To make the conversion, simply multiply the circumference in inches by eight, which means that the equivalent of that old-fashioned three-inch rope is now 3 x 8 = 24mm in diameter.

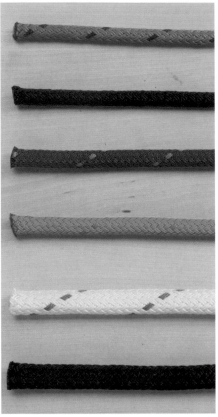

Three-strand matt polyester, used for general moorings, general ropework, locking ropes for narrowboats. Kind to the hands, it coils and splices easily.

6mm   white/blue/red fleck
10mm   burgundy
10mm   white/blue/red fleck
12mm   buff
14mm   green

Three-braid-on-braid polyester. Used for cruising halyards, control lines and sheets, it is very strong, and is low-stretch, flexible and easy to handle.

6mm   orange/purple fleck
8mm   blue/red fleck
8mm   solid navy
10mm   red/blue fleck
10mm   green/blue fleck
12mm   yellow/blue fleck
12mm   black

Braid-on-braid, as previously illustrated, but in different colours.

6mm   white/green fleck
8mm   white/blue fleck
10mm   white/orange fleck
12mm   white/yellow fleck
14mm   white/red fleck
16mm   white

WHAT KNOT?

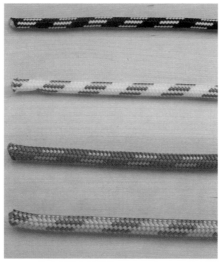

Sixteen-plait polyester sprintline, used for dinghy halyards and control lines. It is hardwearing, strong and has low stretch. It comes in distinctive colours.

6mm	*purple*
6mm	*blue*
5mm	*red*
5mm	*orange*
4mm	*yellow*
4mm	*navy*
3mm	*pink*
3mm	*black*

Dyneemalite, a mix of Dyneema and polypropylene. Used for dinghy sheets and control lines, it is very strong and gives a good grip. It is lightweight and buoyant.

6mm	*black/yellow fleck*
7mm	*yellow/blue fleck*
8mm	*pink/blue fleck*
9mm	*blue/pink fleck*

Eight-plait multifilament polypropylene, used for dinghy sheets, control lines and in buoyancy aids. It is buoyant, strong and holds knots well.

2mm	*white*
3mm	*white*
4mm	*white*
5mm	*black*
6mm	*yellow/red fleck*
8mm	*red/yellow fleck*
10mm	*blue*

INTRODUCTION

SYNTHETIC (MAN-MADE) FIBRES

Almost every kind of cordage is now made from artificial filaments, first developed in laboratories by chemists

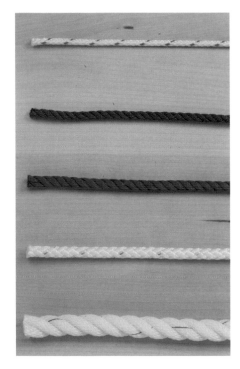

Pre-stretched polyester in three-strand and eight-plait. It is strong and durable with low stretch.
3mm   eight-plait white/orange fleck
4mm   three-strand red/blue fleck
5mm   three-strand blue/red fleck
5mm   eight-plait white/orange fleck
10mm   three-strand white/blue fleck

from the 1930s onwards and available from the 1950s. Predominant are the four Ps: polyamide (known as nylon); polyester (sold as Terylene™ or Dacron™); polyethelene (commonly called polythene); and polypropylene.

Nylon is the strongest, but is 10 to 15 per cent weaker when wet. It was the first to become available commercially. Nylon ropes stretch when loaded, from 10 to 40 per cent, but regain their original form once the load is removed, which makes them suitable for use as towlines, mooring lines and dynamic climbing ropes, when the energy of shock-loading may have to be safely absorbed and dissipated. It can also be used for anchor warps as it does not float.

Terylene and Dacron have about 75 per cent the strength of nylon, wet or dry, and do not stretch nearly as much. Much of the fibre is pre-stretched during manufacture to eliminate latent elasticity, making it suitable for use as guy-lines, and for replacing wire stays on structures where a combination of high tensile strength and an absence of stretch are essential. As polyester remains soft and white, retaining more of its strength and integrity when wet – while nylon absorbs

water, and goes yellow and stiff with age – there is a growing trend towards using polyester for mooring lines, too.

Polythene is not as strong as nylon or terylene, but it is cheap and cheerful, hard-wearing and durable. Used afloat and ashore, both in the fishing industry and agriculture, it is used in a variety of items, from netting to baling twine.

Polypropylene is stronger and lighter than polythene, but comes after nylon and terylene in cost and performance, and is the most versatile of the synthetic fibres. Where exceptional performance is not required, it is the favourite for domestic, industrial and sporting purposes. Like polythene it floats, making it suitable for ski-ropes and life-belt lines.

SUPERFIBRES

The following are too specialized and expensive to practise knots on, but they sometimes become available as used or discarded lengths and off-cuts.

Kevlar™ is the lightest of the state-of-the-art fibres. It is twice as strong as nylon, weight-for-weight, with less stretch than terylene. As its brittle fibres can cut through one another when flexing

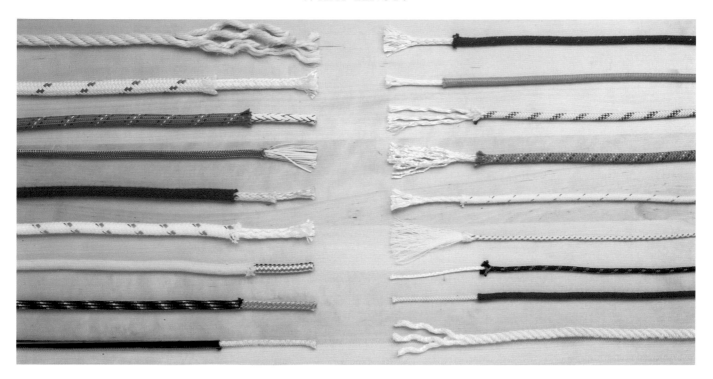

and extending, it is usual to enclose them in a protective sheath made of braided polyester.

Spectra™ is the trade name for Dyneema or HMPE (High Modulus Polyethylene), a super-lightweight product that may supersede Kevlar, in that it is more tolerant to flexing.

Vectran™ is yet another high-performance brand of cordage, does not stretch, and, unlike Kevlar, has the ability to bend around tight radii.

PBO poly(p-phenylene-2,6-benzobisoxazole) is up to 20 per cent stronger than either Vectran or HMPE.

NATURAL FIBRE CORDAGE

All rope and other cordage products were made from natural materials prior to the Second World War, though nowadays they are seen and used less often. However, they still have a place creating nautical interior decorating themes in pubs, clubs and restaurants.

Sheath-on-core (kernmantel)
This selection indicates the variety of sheath-on-core cordage available. Compare the conventional laid cord construction (top left and bottom right) with the different sheath-and-core types. The sheath is always braided, but the core may be of laid cord, continuous and lightly-twisted (but not laid) strands, lightly-twisted and lightly-laid strands, braided in a variety of styles, both hard and soft, or even have a further inner core of its own, as may be seen in the left middle example.

INTRODUCTION

Natural cordage may be used aboard a vintage sailing barge, or in the background of a filmed costume drama in a dockside scene. Soft hemp climbing ropes are still standard equipment in some school gymnasia.

One day soon, perhaps, natural fibre cordage will be possibly adopted by eco-warriors as an alternative to synthetic cordage (at least some of which is a by-product of the oil industry), because much of it is obtained from harvested but renewable crops.

These include flax and jute (from plant stems); abaca or hemp and sisal (from leaves); cotton (from seeds); and coir (from the fibrous husks of coconuts). Other sources of vegetable fibre include date palms, tree bark, reeds and esparto grass.

Materials of animal origin include hair (from camels, horses and human beings), gut, silk and wool.

Hemp is one of the strongest and most durable of the ropes made from natural fibre, but manila has greater resistance to rot when wet, while sisal is a cheap substitute for both. Coir is elastic and can withstand immersion in salt water, although it has only a quarter of the strength of manila, which is why it is made into what is known as 'grass rope' for throwing lines, and is fitted to some traditional hire boats and other small craft in the form of fenders.

COMPARING & CONTRASTING SYNTHETIC AND NATURAL FIBRE CORDAGE

Natural fibre cordage swells when wet, jamming any knots that may be tied in it. Wet ropes can freeze, causing brittle fibres to snap when bent, and irreparably weakening affected strands. They have to be carefully dried before they can be stowed away, otherwise they will be prone to mildew and rot, while insects and vermin are likely to chew on them at any time. From a decorative point of view, they are drab. Colours – with the exception of white cotton (for posh yachts and some barrier ropes in banks and building societies, cinemas and cafeterias) are limited to a range that goes from flaxen-blonde to dark-brown. If natural fibre cordage is used in ornamental ropework, it will need to be painted to make a colourful display.

Nevertheless, older ropeworkers still retain an affection for the evocative smell and feel of Italian tarred hemp, manila from the Philippines, sisal from the Yucután Peninsula of Central American, coir from the Malabar coast or Ceylon, and Egyptian cotton.

In contrast, synthetics can be put away wet, being unlikely to rot or be affected by mildew. Nylon and terylene are especially good not only at withstanding abrasion but also exposure to alkaline chemicals. Acid damages nylon more easily than it does terylene, and so does UV radiation from sunlight.

Synthetic cordage melts when fiercely heated, while its surface will glaze and harden at the lower temperatures generated by friction, impairing its performance. Nylon and terylene have the highest melting points at about 245°C (473°F), with polypropylene and polythene much lower at about 150°C (302°F) and 128°C (262°F) respectively.

For the fancy knot enthusiast, synthetic cordage comes in brilliant white and black, as well as vivid primary colours, also silver and gold, rainbow hues, fluorescent pink and psychedelic mixtures. It is now commonplace to have colour-coded sheets and halyards aboard racing dinghies and yachts.

CONSTRUCTION

Rope, either of synthetic or natural fibre, that consists of a number of spiral strands, is referred to as hawser-laid and when the strands are seen spiralling clockwise as the rope recedes from the viewer's eye, it is said to be right-handed or Z-laid. Each strand is composed of many yarns which have been twisted counter-clockwise, when they are said to be left-handed or S-laid. This twist and counter-twist combine to create the rope's characteristic geometry, flexibility and strength.

Three such hawsers may be laid up, left-handed, into a thicker cable, when it is referred to as cable-laid. Hawsers can also be made using S-laid or left-handed strands, when their constituent yarns must be Z-laid or right-handed; a cable made from them would, of course, be right-handed.

Natural fibres are comparatively short and irregular, so that even when sorted, graded and combed by the ropemaker, the cordage made from them will be correspondingly weak and hairy.

Synthetic ropes, on the other hand, are made from endless extruded monofilaments (or bundles of finer multi-filaments) of a uniform cross-section throughout, with the result that they are stronger and smoother than natural fibre ropes. Early products were so slippery as to make some old, tried-and-trusted knots insecure and unreliable. Therefore, knot manuals reprinted from that period usually recommend adding extra tucks and hitches in order to secure them. Now, however, more knots have appeared that can cope with synthetic cordage, and many such products now have a matt finish, making them ideal for knotting. Today, ropemakers are aware of the need to create user-friendly products, and have incorporated a percentage of short monofilaments which, when made into rope, recreate the lost fuzziness of natural fibre. This cordage is described and sold as staple-spun.

Also available are three-stranded polyester ropes with a matt finish, dyed to resemble a hemp-like natural fibre, which will not rot or degrade, absorb water, swell, shrink or lose its strength.

Another synthetic product is made from polypropylene film, shredded, combed and twisted into what are known as split-film ropes.

INTRODUCTION

Most synthetic cordage today is not laid, but is either plaited or has an outer covering or sheath made up from 8, 16 or 32 bundles of parallel monofilaments or multifilaments braided around a core. This core may be laid, plaited, lightly twisted or straight. Cordage of this kind is collectively known as sheath-and-core or braid-on-braid. Climbing ropes are sometimes referred to by their European designation of kernmantel (literally: core-sheath).

Occasionally the core is itself a sheath surrounding a second innermost core – a sort of braid-on-braid-on-braid.

Braided rope that lacks a core is called hollow-braid.

Braid-on-braid is the strongest of the cordage constructions. A braided polyester outer cover and an almost parallel polyester core work in unison to achieve maximum strength and low-stretch with excellent durability. This kind of rope is hard-wearing and achieves rapid response when used, for example, as control lines aboard a sailing dinghy.

The enormous strength-to-weight ratio of Kevlar enables it to be used in smaller, lighter cordage, provided the brittle fibres are enclosed in a protective sheath of tough polyester. The liquid-crystal polymer, Vectran, is another of the superfibres that is enclosed in a polyester sheath to combine optimum strength and durability. Nylon's tendency to stretch can be reduced by containing it within a polyester sheath of limited elasticity. Alternatively, it can be retained and its strength enhanced by means of an eight-strand plaited cable

Woven nylon or polypropylene tape or webbing is made in two forms: either flat (as in seat-belts for motor vehicles) or tubular (like a flattened hose-pipe). Treated like flat rope it can also be knotted, and it is used to make the specialized belts, harnesses and slings used by climbers. It also makes effective straps for roof racks holding holiday luggage, and is useful in surfboards and canoes, and as trailer straps for boats, motorbikes and gliders. There are even acid-resistant webbing straps for batteries.

Shock (or bungee) cords are constructed using a high-grade elastic core made from natural rubber enclosed in a polyester cover. A clever application is to use them to test the security of knots; many knots wriggle and slip out of shock elastics, while others cling and hold firm. A bowline (page 82) will come apart in a second, but the angler's or perfection loop (page 47) beds down snugly and stays put. When circumnavigating the Isle of Wight, off the south coast of England in a sea kayak, with deck elastics holding chart, drink bottle and waterproofs, tied with a number of these knots, they held fast, even though sea-soaked, sun-dried and swamped repeatedly by waves, and they untied readily at the end of the journey. Similarly, while the sheet bend is likely to perform poorly, a Simple Simon (pages 96–97) is more likely to impress.

NOTE General-purpose cordage bought from a local DIY or camping shop will not have the same performance criteria built into them as the more costly type sold in specialist outdoor activities stores and yacht chandleries. Potential buyers and users requiring detailed performance specifications, including breaking and safe working loads, can obtain this information from rope manufacturers and reputable retailers.

WHAT KNOT?

BREAKING LOAD

This is the manufacturer's calculation or estimate, expressed in kilograms or tonnes, of the load a rope will sustain before failing. It disregards factors such as wear and tear, or the inclusion of knots, which may drastically reduce this figure. Shock loading, be it the jerking of a towing vehicle taking up slack, or a falling climber, will also multiply the load by the factor of acceleration, and may cause a rope to break. Nevertheless, the best synthetic cords and ropes are capable of great feats of strength which, depending upon materials and constructions, can range from 112lb (50kg) for a 1-mm diameter polypropylene cord, to an astonishing 134 tons (17,000kg for a 20-mm Dyneema rope.

SAFE WORKING LOAD

This is the estimated load, often as little as one fifth or less of the actual breaking load, that a rope may be certified to withstand, taking into account various weakening factors.

The only way to add muscle to natural fibre cordage was to increase its circumference. Try to visit a maritime

museum, where it is possible to see the massive 24-inch anchor warps and other unwieldy cordage that was constucted as a result. Even so, such ropes were barely up to the tasks assigned to them and it was necessary to use every trick in the book to preserve their limited strength. As knots were known to drastically weaken ropes, and were impossible to tie in the thickest ones, it was the practice to prefer splices to knots whenever possible.

Today, synthetic cordage is slimmer yet often stronger than needed for the work required of it, and some knots approach 100 per cent efficiency. Consequently, although splices do have their uses, they are no longer the automatic solution to every ropeworking problem. Back splices and eye splices are easy enough to tie in hawser-laid ropes (pages 232–233 and 234–235), but splicing sheath-and-core cordage is a more fiddly and time-consuming process, requiring specialized tools and not a little patience. It is best done with the aid of the instruction sheets provided by cordage manufacturers and retailers; meanwhile, a knotted alternative can be contrived in seconds.

INTRODUCTION

For instance, the scaffold knot (pages 128–129) makes an excellent 'hard eye', that is, one reinforced by a metal or plastic thimble, and will also enable a tackle to be pulled block-to-block, when a longer eye splice can restrict the range of movement in that same tackle.

CARE OF CORDAGE

Cordage can be costly, so take good care of it. Never leave cut ends to fray and unravel – they can never be restored. Fraying can be avoided in hawser-laid ropes by quickly and easily back-splicing them. Aternatively, cut ends can be wrapped with adhesive tape, bound with whipping twine, or heat-sealed.

This can be done quickly and neatly with the blade of a pocket knife that has been heated in a flame, or by means of either a hand-held or table-top electric guillotine. For a rough-and-ready job, many knot tyers keep a disposable cigarette lighter handy – whether or not they actually smoke – especially for the purpose. A lighter with an adjustable flame, like a mini-DIY blowtorch, will cope with all sorts of thick cords or thin twines. This treatment is referred to humorously as a 'butane whipping' or, if matches are used, a 'Bryant & May (or a Swan Vesta) splice'.

The following should also be observed:

Do not needlessly expose any cordage to bright sunlight.

Do keep all cordage (synthetics in particular) away from bleach, battery acid and any other chemical contamination.

Do not allow synthetics to generate heat through friction. Avoid ill-fitting blocks, cleats and fairleads and do not drag them over or around sharp angles.

Do keep ropes away from barbecues, spark-spitting camp fires, acetylene-torches and even lighted matches.

Do not tread on a rope, drop it from a height, or allow it to become nipped, twisted, cockled or kinked.

Do coil rope loosely and hang in up above ground level when not in use.

Do not allow wet ropes to freeze.

Do store all ropes in a dark, dry place with adequate air circulation and a relative humidity between 40–60 per cent.

Do not wash ropes with harsh detergents in washing machines.

When needed, do hand-wash grubby

cordage using mild soap to remove grit and grime and the salt crystals left behind by seawater.

Do not, however, be afraid to use your cordage. It must work to justify the outlay expended on it. Fair wear and tear is inevitable, but its working life can be extended by turning lines end-to-end when wear becomes apparent in a particular place.

INSPECTING CORDAGE

Any rope that is to be used in circumstances where its failure could result in damage or loss, personal injury or death, should be inspected periodically. Metre by metre or yard by yard, make sure you are in a good light, then look for worn and broken or frayed surface yarns or filaments and cut strands. Some surface fluffing is unavoidable and may actually protect the rope from further wear. Look for staining and softening due to chemical attack, as well as visible evidence of heat-damage.

NOTE If the rope has become attenuated and weakened by stretching, with the result that it has become

smaller in diameter and with a more acute angle of lay in the grooves between the strands, twist apart the strands of each hawser-laid rope to check for internal wear or damage.

A sheath-and-core rope conceals its innards, but undesirable 'creep' may become apparent if the sheath moves separately over the heart strands. Otherwise, some sort of risk assessment must be made based upon the rope's history of use, misuse and possible abuse. A written log is recommended for each and every climbing rope, as well as those used in lifting tackles. Prolonged heavy usage, or maybe a single instance of extreme overload, should result in a rope either being discarded or downgraded to less demanding work. Use it instead for learning, practising and teaching knots.

TOOLS

Every knot in this book can be tied using only the fingers, unaided by any tool. Tools help, however, when it comes to tucking ends through tight spaces, tightening knots, concealing the loose ends of ornamental knots, such as the Turk's head (pages 214–219), and for

pulling apart knots that have been heavily loaded. Ropeworking tools are few and basic but somewhat unusual. Here is a selection:

Knife: Something is needed to cut both cords and ropes, and scissors can only cope with the weaker and thinner type of cordage. For everything else, a keen pocket knife, a razor-sharp craft knife and a pair of snips or shears are indispensable.

Fids: These are tapered hardwood spikes, usually round when seen in cross-section, which are used for poking and prodding stubborn splices and other recalcitrant pieces of knotwork. Hand-held fids are somewhere between 6 and 12 inches (15 and 30cm) long.

Swedish fids: The name originated in the 1950s, when their prototypes bore the legend, 'Made in Sweden', but it is now a generic term used for any such tool. A Swedish fid is made from stainless steel, is half-round in cross-section and hollow, and ends in a rounded handgrip. The business end tapers to a point but, unlike a solid fid, which must be removed before a tuck can be achieved in the space gained, a Swedish fid provides a channel into which the w'end can be laid, trapped by the user's thumb. It is then pulled through as the tool is withdrawn.

Gripspikes: These modified Swedish fids trap and pull a strand or working end, so that a restraining thumb is no longer needed. The original models were devised and produced by Stuart Grainger of the IGKT in the 1980s and have proved so adaptable that weavers and other textile craftsmen have adopted and adapted them for their own use. A few users now make their own, but one day they will possibly be mass-produced.

Marlinspikes (Marlinespikes or Marlingspikes): These are hand-held metal spikes used for tough splicing jobs and also as levers to heave tight various bindings, lashings and seizings. The bulbous head can be used to pound handiwork into shape.

Prickers: These are small marlinspikes that are sometimes fitted with wooden handles.

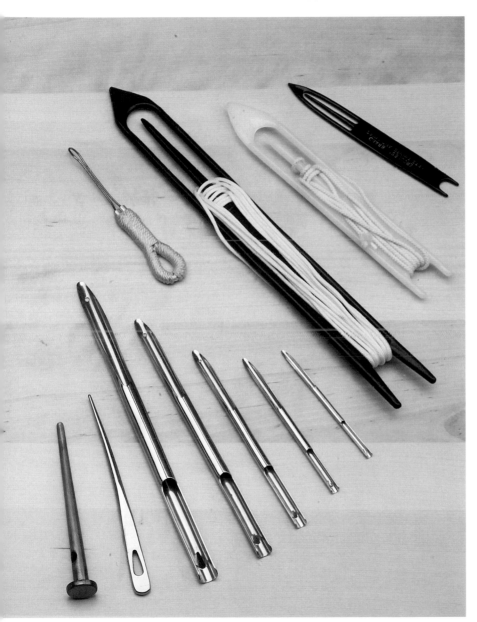

Wire loops: Most exponents of fancy knots have several different sizes of these home-made tools, each consisting of a springy piece of piano wire, bent in half and securely inserted into a handle. They are used to pull, tuck and bury ends. As the strand or end must be tugged through doubled, this can at times prove awkward. Where a wire loop does not work, a hollow needle will probably complete the job.

Needles (hollow): These items are designed to grip and hold a working end or other strand, so as to thread, tuck, splice or bury it. Unlike a wire loop, the diameter of the join is no larger than that of the needle itself, into which the cord end has been simply inserted. Some have an internal thread into which the line is actually screwed. Either way, it can be pushed and pulled through tightly-laid or knotted structures. These needles are made of metal or plastic and come in a range of sizes. The component parts of larger commercial sets nest and stow neatly inside one another.

Tools for knots and splices.

INTRODUCTION

Needles (various): Domestic, industrial, straight or curved, all sorts of needles often come in handy. The cross-section of a sailmaker's needle is triangular.

Sailmaker's palm: Designed to protect the hand as it pushes the needle through sail canvas, the palm also comes into its own whenever tough stitching through knot-work has to be done. Left-handed versions are also obtainable.

Round-billed pliers (large or small): When fingers alone are not strong enough to complete the job, use these for tightening knots or loosening them.

Netting needles: Apart from making a net, these implements come in handy for storing string, twine and small-diameter cords. They can be bought, or home-made, in a range of sizes from a slim and short 4 inches (10cm) to a jumbo-sized 12 inches (30cm) long.

It is possible, from time to time, for knot-tyers to acquire the discarded tools of other trades and professions, either from boot and garage sales or from eBay. These could be anything from a pair of end-cutting pliers, designed for repairing manual typewriters, to a streamlined and stylish implement made of stainless steel and ideal for fancy knotting that was once a former surgical instrument.

BASIC KNOTTING TERMS & TECHNIQUES

The parts of a length of line in which a knot is tied, with its various twists and tucks, all have names. The end employed in tying the knot is the working end (which some knot-tyers cut-and-shut to w'end or wend). The inactive end is the standing end (st'end or stend) and everything in between is the standing part. Any curve in a line of less than 180°, resembling a shallow bay on a coastline map, is a bight. In the past, anything with a bend greater than that was called an open loop, but knotting evolves and terms mutate, so that nowadays this too tends to be called a bight. When the two legs of a bight or open loop touch or form a crossing point it became a closed loop, or simply a loop. When using the working end to form a loop, if it goes on top of the crossing point, it is an overhand loop and if it goes beneath, then it is an underhand loop. When a loop is left protruding in the form of a bow from any knot, as a method of quick-release for easy untying, the knot is said to be a slipped knot (as opposed to a slip-knot which is a simple noose or snare) and the loop itself is a draw-loop.

Very few knots can be tightened by merely pulling on one end or another. Careless or impatient tightening by pulling and tugging at a knot, leaving intrusive kinks and twists, will mar its final appearance, and could weaken or destabilize it. The deft knot-tyer neatly rearranges each loosely completed knot, dressing it, then carefully eliminating unwanted daylight by removing any slackness, then snugging it, prior to a final tightening with fingers, spike or pliers.

Knots: Strictly speaking, a knot is anything that is not a bend or a hitch. This includes bindings, shortenings, stoppers, loops and nooses, as well as numerous mavericks and mutations, both plain and fancy. Many loop knots are used as hitches, because they can be applied, removed, then reapplied with no need to tie, untie and retie them.

Anything tied in string or thinner

cord is generally referred to as a knot, even though it may behave like a bend or hitch. The fisherman's knot (page 49), for example, is a joining knot or bend named long ago by anglers, who used it in fishing lines made of gut, horsehair or silk. These snippets of arcane lore are all part of the enchantment of knotting as far as its devotees are concerned. Then again, it is perfectly alright to refer to any bend or hitch as a knot.

Strangers to knotting sometimes assume it must be an '-ology' and wish to know which one. Tell them funicology, ligatology, nodology or vincology, all of which are of Latin derivation. Alternatively, if you prefer Greek, tell them desmology, kompology, plektology, schoinology or sunnamology. Mind you, no knot-tyer would dream of uttering any one of these pretentious words, but we quite like the tongue-in-cheek knottology, and sometimes refer to ourselves as knottologists in fun.

Bends: When two separate ropes are knotted, rather than spliced, because they are intended they be taken apart again later, they are said to be 'bent together'.

Hitches: These attach ropes to a hook, post, ring, rail, spar or another rope. Most are intended to cope with a load that pulls more or less at right angles to the point of attachment. Some are designed to withstand a pull that varies its direction, while others can deal with a lengthwise pull. The anchor bend (page 58) is a hitch, its name being a reminder that sailors once upon a time spoke of 'bending' a rope to a ring.

NAMES OF KNOTS

Alpine butterfly, Simple Simon, Zeppelin bend – they sound like acrobatic feats performed by competitive Olympic divers, or exotic cocktails consumed in smart bistro-bars, or maybe disastrous computer viruses, but in fact these are just three of the multifarious knots known and tied today. Knots are named in one or other of several ways according to their use, their user, their appearance, their association with, their nationality, their use by a person, their characteristics or simply to be whimsical. Examples are as follows:

Use: Bottle sling; handcuff knot; heaving line bend.

INTRODUCTION

User: Artilleryman's loop; hangman's noose; stevedore knot.

Appearance: Figure-of-eight knot; round turn and two half hitches; tricorn loop.

Association (real or assumed): Scout coil; oysterman's stopper; Zeppelin bend.

Nationality: Flemish bend; Italian hitch; Spanish bowline.

Person: Hunter's bend; Matthew Walker's knot; Tarbuck knot.

Characteristic: Constrictor knot; frustrator; snuggle hitch.

Whimsy: Pedigree cow hitch; perfection loop; Simple Simon.

Some knots are nameless, while others have more than one name, so that one person may call a knot one thing, while the other knows it as something else. It is not necessary to know the name of a knot in order to tie and use it. When meeting and talking with other knot-tyers, or consulting knot books, the names of knots can either clarify or confuse a issue.

KNOT SELECTION & PERFORMANCE

The type of cordage in which a knot is tied affects its performance, which can be summed up in terms of the three Ss, namely stability, security and strength.

Stability: This is the test of a knot's behaviour when it is subjected to an abnormal load. Does it deform, capsize or spill? If so, then it must be watched closely while in use, or another knot used instead.

Security: Some knots jam when heavily loaded, making them difficult, if not impossible, to undo, while others hang together loosely and can be easily untied. Somewhere in between are the knots which slip a bit, absorbing and dissipating dangerous load energy before holding firm. All of these factors affect a knot's strength.

Strength: Most knots weaken the cord or rope in which they occur. An overhand knot (page 38), for instance, causes the rope to break at half its theoretical breaking strength; therefore, with an efficiency of barely 50 per cent, the knot can be said to be 'weak', though 'cruelty' or 'unkindness' to the cordage may be a more accurate description. Many knots are rated at 80 per cent or more, while a few can claim 100 per cent.

The lighterman's mooring hitch (pages 194–195) is very strong and secure, yet can be cast off in a few life-saving seconds. The frustrator (page 114), on the other hand, resists efforts to untie it, hence its name. Choosing the right knot for the job is often a compromise, where it is necessary to sacrifice some of one quality for more of another. For example, the common bowline (page 82) enjoys the soubriquet 'King of Knots', although it is not particularly strong or secure. If used as a life-support knot, it must be reinforced with extra turns and tucks; but yachtsmen and women will not tolerate this afloat, since it is one they may have to release in a hurry.

What practical knots should a beginner learn first? It is debatable. Ask any experienced knot-tyer, however, and certain knots come up repeatedly. These include the constrictor knot; the figure-of-eight knot (which can be adapted to act as a stopper knot, bend, hitch or loop); the round turn and two half hitches; the bowline; the sheet bend; and the buntline hitch, all of which will be discussed.

TYING TIPS

It is natural to attempt to tie a new knot with a working end (or ends). Some knots must be tied in the slack standing portion of a line, without using either end, and these are said to be tied 'in the bight', while others that are tied with an end can also be tied in the bight.

The law of loop, hitch & bight

Tying knots in the bight is generally quicker and more impressive to watch, in that its execution seems to be almost a feat of legerdemain. To discover if a knot can be tied in the bight, try to locate and then withdraw a key locking part of that knot. Any knot that falls apart to leave only a memory of itself – 'untying from the bight' – can invariably be tied in the bight. This is the litmus test that enables us to determine whether or not any knot can be tied in the bight. For instance, the knots used in parcelling techniques, known as half-hitching (page 61) and marline-hitching (page 62) appear to be identical, but slide each one off its foundations, and it will be noticed that the half-hitching collapses to nothing, and therefore can be tied in the bight, while the marline-hitching produces a series of linked overhand knots, indicating that to tie it needs an end. The constrictor knot (pages 110–111) can be tied in the bight, but a strangle knot (page 126) cannot. This law

of loop, hitch and bight was first proposed by Dr. Harry Asher in *A New System of Knotting, Volume 2*, published in 1986 by the IGKT.

The ability to tie a knot, either with an end or in the bight, has practical applications. Take the angler's loop (page 47), for example. To attach it to a ring or around a rail, it must be tied with an end; otherwise it is more fluently tied in the bight. Some knots can be tied in several different ways. The techniques described and illustrated in this book have been chosen either because they are easy to learn or illustrate. Having learned to tie a knot, it is often worthwhile to play around with it and find other ways of tying it which may suit you better.

Do/Undo

The idea that knots are best learned by untying them, once you have tied them in the first place, came from the fertile brain of Harry Asher. It is also a way of discovering other methods of tying knots.

The Parsimony Principle

To the uninitiated, many knots look alike and half hitches and marline hitches have already been mentioned in this context.

The sheet bend (page 91) and bowline (page 82) also seem identical, though they are deployed differently. In fact, just a few twists and turns and crossing points go to make up a wide variety of knots, bends and hitches. This implies there is a parsimonious (mean or miserly) aspect to knotting, but by mastering and then combining a few basic knotting manoeuvres, more complicated knots can be assembled.

MIRROR IMAGES

Most, if not all knots, have mirror images of themselves. Just as cordage can be left-handed or right-handed (S-laid or Z-laid), so knots can also appear in one or another of two versions of opposite-handedness. If any one of the knots in this book seems awkward or unnatural, hold it up to a mirror and see how its reflection looks. Then attempt to reproduce it. It may be that your hands and your brain prefer the other version.

CHAPTER ONE

OVERHAND KNOTS,
HALF-KNOTS
& HALF HITCHES

'In fact, knots are often better and more logically arranged and studied according to their structure than according to the purposes for which they are used.'

From Charles Warner's
A Fresh Approach to Knotting and Ropework, 1992

Being able to tie knots is not a gift, it is a reward, and should you decide to learn the knots in this section, and in the sections that follow, then you will be able to recall them next month, next year, and in ten years' time. A knot that is forgotten was never properly learned in the first place. Knots are for life.

If there is a knot that everyone can tie, and never had to be taught it, it must be the simple overhand or thumb knot. Indeed it can tie itself in discarded coils of rope, garden hosepipes, clothes lines or bits and pieces of string lying in a drawer; and while this is an inconvenience, the overhand knot can also be used intentionally as a stopper knot, to prevent an end from pulling free or unravelling, when it would be undesirable for it to do so.

Although seemingly simple, this is actually a trefoil knot. Tie it around an object and it forms a half-knot, with either a left-handed or right-handed twist, or a half hitch – the choice is yours. From an angler's loop to the fireman's chair knot and a bend for mooring lighter-than-air ships, the overhand knot and its two siblings are the basis of them all.

Alternatively, tuck the working end once or twice more to obtain the double- and triple-overhand knots, then mix-and-match these muscular variations to create stronger, more secure bends or bindings, hitches, loops and shortenings, many of which feature in later sections.

OVERHAND KNOTS, HALF-KNOTS & HALF HITCHES

OVERHAND or THUMB KNOT

Use this as a quick and easy stopper knot in the ends of sewing thread, string and twine, cord and small ropes, to prevent them from either fraying or pulling through from some anchorage point. Put loose change in one corner of a handkerchief, then tie this knot to keep the coins together – useful for keeping money safe in a leisure centre locker or when changing on a beach.

In the days before fashionable leisure wear, men used to tie an overhand knot in each of the four corners of a large handkerchief to improvise a sun hat. While it was probably not a safe barrier against harmful UV radiation, it remains a trick worth knowing as a short-term measure, should you be caught without a hat on a hot, sunny day.

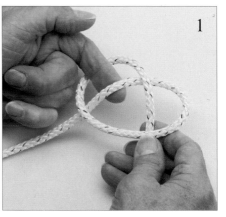
1

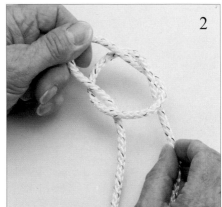
2

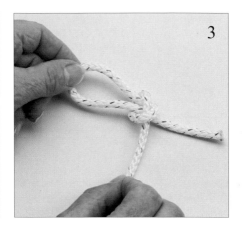
3

1 With the working end, form an overhand loop.

2 Begin to pull the w'end through the loop from behind.

3 Stop at this stage, and if you wish to retain a draw-loop for easy untying later, tighten the resulting knot.

4 Otherwise, pull the w'end right through and tighten the knot so that it lies more or less at right angles to its standing part.

4

DOUBLE-OVERHAND KNOT

This makes a neater stopper knot for all sorts of smaller cordages, as the working end remains in line with the standing part. It will not block a hole larger than a simple overhand or thumb knot, however.

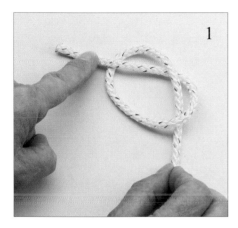

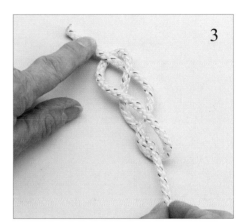

1 Tie an overhand knot.

2 Take an extra tuck with the w'end.

3 Now pull w'end and st'end apart, twiddling them in opposite directions (in this instance, counter-clockwise) so that a diagonal wrapping turn is created.

4 Tighten the resulting knot so that it lies at right angles to its standing part.

TRIPLE-OVERHAND KNOT

This knot is a more ornamental version of the preceding ones, but will not stop or block a larger hole.

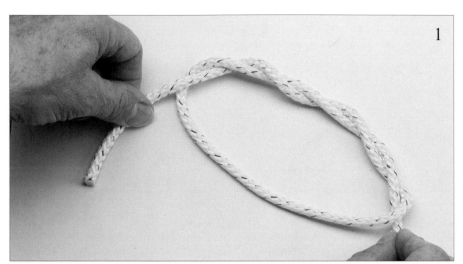

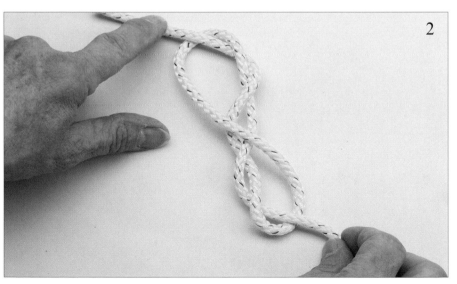

NOTE *Take more than three initial tucks and depending upon how many are made, a four-fold, five-fold or bigger multiple overhand knot will emerge. These are known collectively as 'blood knots', perhaps because they resemble the knots tied by surgeons in sutures, or maybe because they were once tied in cat-o'-nine-tails to lacerate the victim's skin. They can be seen more commonly in the ropes some orders of nuns and monks wear around their waists.*

1 Tie the familiar overhand or thumb knot.

2 Take two extra tucks.

3 Pull and twiddle (as already described). Tighten.

OVERHAND SHORTENING

There are two main uses for this knotty contrivance: it temporarily shortens any length of round cordage or flat tape/webbing that is too long for the task in hand. Then again, it can form twin fixed leg loops or other attachment points in a climbing harness. It can also be used to create a couple of clip-on points in any kind of safety line.

1 Fold or pleat the tape/webbing, cord or rope into three parts.

2,3 Using all three, tie a simple overhand or thumb knot.

4 Tighten, taking care to eliminate needless twists or cross-overs.

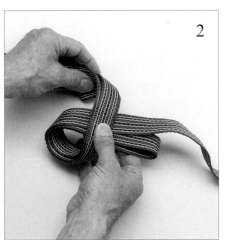

BOATING & SAILING

OUTDOOR PURSUITS

CAVING & CLIMBING

FROST KNOT

This knot is specifically designed to make the loops from which to suspend the short looped stirrups or climbing ladders called étriers.

The knot was named after Tom Frost, who is credited by climbers to have been its originator in the 1960s.

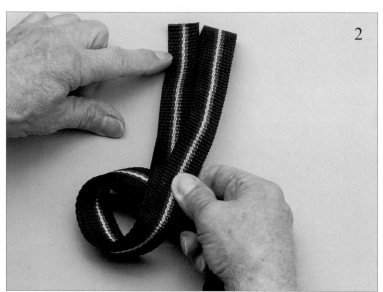

1 Bring the two ends of a length of tape/webbing together, one of them doubled over, with the other placed inside it.

2, 3 Tie an overhand knot in the three thicknesses. Tighten, leaving a knotted loop of the required size.

OVERHAND LOOP

*This is a general-purpose, come-in-handy fixed loop
for both tape/webbing and round cordage.*

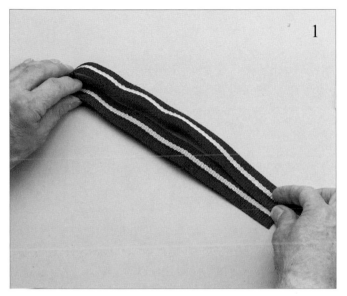

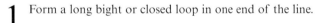

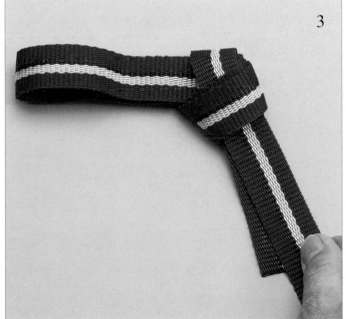

1 Form a long bight or closed loop in one end of the line.

2 Tie a simple overhand or thumb knot in the doubled
portion.

3 Tighten the resulting knot, taking care to eliminate any
ugly and undesirable twists or cross-overs.

BLOOD-KNOT LOOP or SURGEON'S KNOT

This is a stronger fixed loop than the overhand loop, but is suitable only for twines and thinner cords.

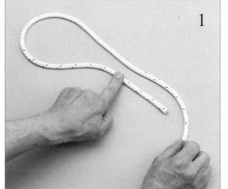

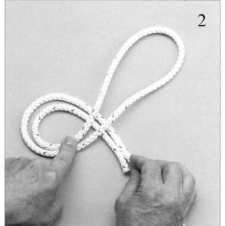

4 Take an extra tuck and begin to tighten the knot as if making a double-overhand knot.

5 Tighten, taking care to remove undesirable twists or cross-overs.

Tied with more than two tucks, this knot makes a strong loop for nylon fishing line.

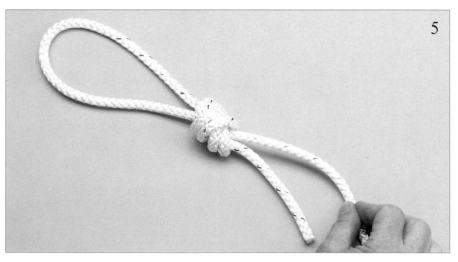

1 Form a long bight or closed loop in one end of the line.

2,3 Tie an overhand knot with the doubled portion.

SIMPLE NOOSE

*Use this simplest of sliding loops to begin any sort of lashing
or parcelling.*

1 Hold the short end and begin to tie a
simple overhand or thumb knot with
the standing part of the cord or string.

2 Draw out a loop of roughly the
required size.

3 Tighten.

TRICORN LOOP

This is a good-looking fixed loop with each face, back and front, in the form of a three-part crown.

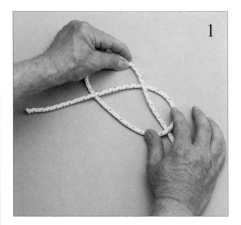

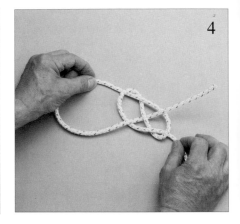

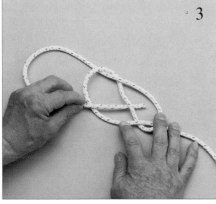

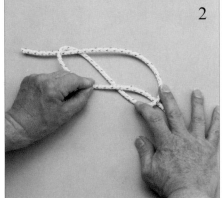

3,4 Take the working end and insert it over-under-over in a locking tuck.

5 Pull the standing part and the upper loop leg in opposite directions until the knot capsizes into its final form. Then tighten it.

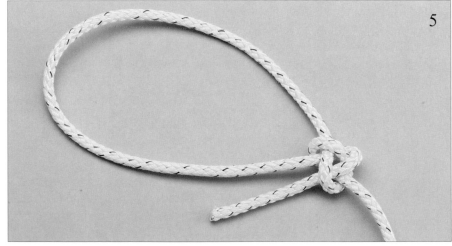

1 Tie a simple overhand or thumb knot, in this instance, right-handed or Z-laid.

2 Deform the knot (as shown) into the shape of a false figure of eight.

ANGLER'S or PERFECTION LOOP

This fixed loop, once only known to anglers, has crossed over into the world of cordage knots, where it is well-suited to synthetic stuff of all kinds. It will even hold fast in shock elastics (bungee cords), which shrug off otherwise dependable knots such as the bowline. To tie the angler's or perfection loop in the bight, see Chapter 5 (Wrap-&-Tuck Knots) on page 127. Attachment to a ring or other fixed anchorage point, however, necessitates tying it with an end.

1 Tie a simple overhand or thumb knot and pass the working end though a ring or other point of attachment.

2 Tuck the w'end back through the belly of the knot, as if to form a draw-loop.

3 Then take the w'end up behind the standing part of the line and insert it down through the knot as shown.

4 Tighten the knot, then turn it over to discover its other distinctive side.

As the name of this knot suggests, it was once upon a time used to make a terminal loop in fishing lines of gut, horsehair or silk.

BAG, SACK or MILLER'S KNOT

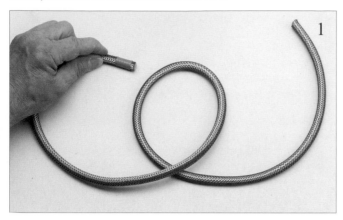

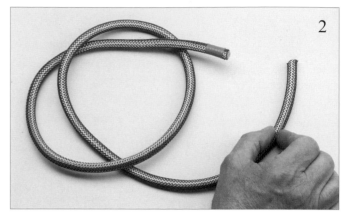

1,2 With one end of a short length of lashing, tie a simple overhand or thumb knot.

3 Take hold of the other w'end and tuck it up around the back of the first end, then over and down through the knot already formed.

4 Place the knot around the neck of the sack to be secured and tighten it.

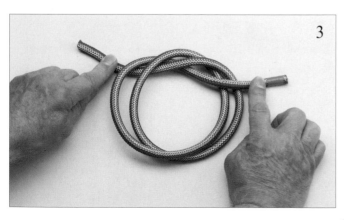

WHAT KNOT?

FISHERMAN'S KNOT

Use this to join together any two lengths of cordage (twine, string, cord or rope) of similar diameter and construction. It is a compact knot, with both working ends lying neatly alongside their adjacent standing parts.

This is an angling knot that has crossed over from old-fashioned fishing lines of gut, horsehair and silk to work effectively in both natural fibre and synthetic cordage.

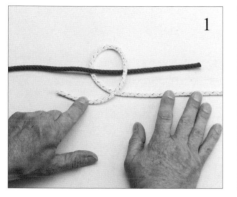 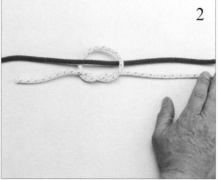 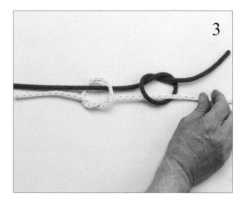

1 With one w'end, tie a simple overhand or thumb knot around the standing part of the other line.

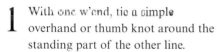

2,3 With the other w'end, tie a second overhand knot around the other standing part. Both knots should be identical – that is, either left-handed/S-laid (as illustrated) or right-handed/Z-laid.

4,5 Tighten the individual knots, at the same time pulling them together. Discover the other distinctive face of this knot.

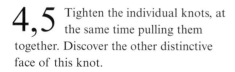

Reverse side

TAPE/WEBBING KNOT

This tough bend also works well in round cordage.

This is another old-time angling knot, known as the 'water knot', which was tied in fishing lines of gut, horsehair or silk.

BOATING & SAILING

OUTDOOR PURSUITS

CAVING & CLIMBING

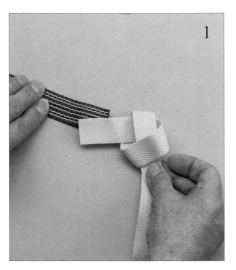

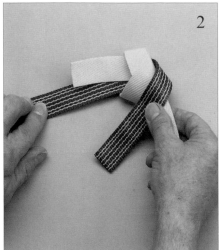

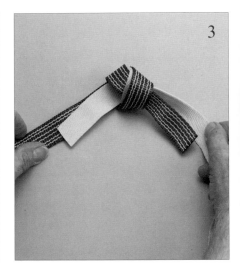

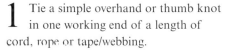

1 Tie a simple overhand or thumb knot in one working end of a length of cord, rope or tape/webbing.

2 Insert the other w'end through the belly of the knot.

3 Follow the original lead faithfully around with the second w'end.

4 Tighten the resulting knot, taking care to eliminate any unwanted twists or cross-overs, so that both cords or ropes act like a railway track, and the two pieces of tape/webbing resemble a necktie knot.

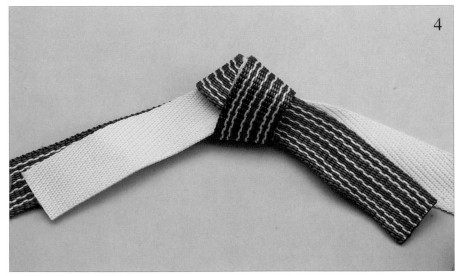

WHAT KNOT?

HUNTER'S BEND

This is one of a family of knots (see also the Zeppelin Bend on page 52), all the members of which consist of two overhand knots interlinked one way or another.

The American, Phil D. Smith, invented this bend on the San Francisco waterfront in the 1940s, during the Second World War, but it was rediscovered and widely publicized by the English physician, Dr. Edward Hunter, in 1978. The media coverage of this knot led to the formation of the International Guild of Knot Tyers in 1982.

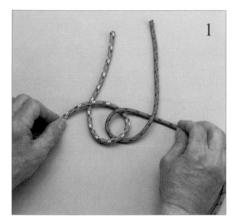

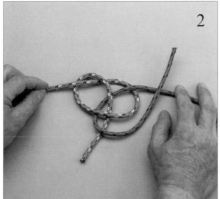

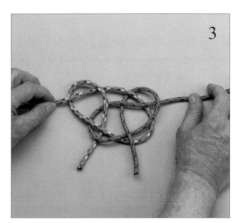

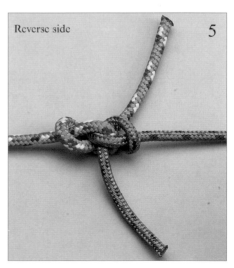

1 With the two working ends, form twin interlocking loops (one underhand, the other overhand) as shown.

2 Tuck the left hand w'end forward and down through both loops.

3 Tuck the right-hand w'end down behind to emerge up through both loops.

4,5 Tighten the resulting knot. Turn the knot over to discover its other distinctive face.

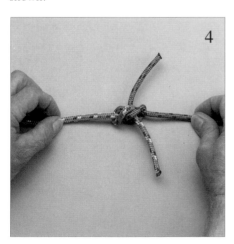

ZEPPELIN BEND

This is a strong and secure bend that should be used more often. It is easily taken apart, even after heavy intermittent or sustained loading. In the event of a load being introduced prematurely, however, while the knot is still loose, it tends to tighten itself rather than pull apart.

The heroic U.S. naval officer and aeronaut, Charles Rosendahl, who in the 1930s commanded the massive dirigible, U.S.S. Los Angeles, only allowed this bend to be used to join his craft's mooring lines to the ground ropes. The navy continued to use the knot for its lighter-than-air ships until 1967.

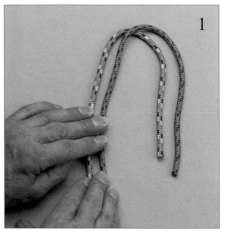

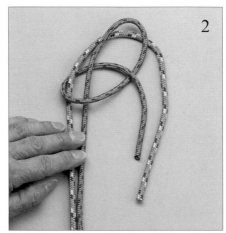

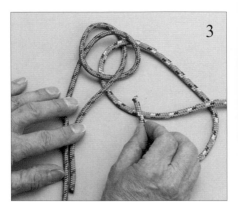

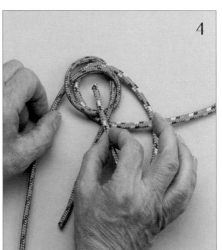

1 Hold the two ends to be joined as shown.

2 With the working end that lies on top (or in front), tie a half hitch around both standing parts.

3 Next bring the lower standing part across in front of its own w'end.

4 Bring that w'end up and tuck it down through the middle of the resulting knot, alongside the first w'end but pointing in the opposite direction.

5 Tighten the knot.

WHAT KNOT?

REEF KNOT

This is strictly a binding knot, tied in both ends of the same length of lace or lashing, and should never be used as a bend. It works best in bandages and parcels (including reefed sails), when the knot presses against whatever it has been tied around.

BOATING & SAILING
HOUSE & GARDEN
CAVING & CLIMBING

NOTE A reef knot with twin draw-loops creates a double reef bow, which is the most secure way of tying shoelaces. If half-knots of the same handedness are used, then a double granny bow will result, and the shoelace is more likely to come undone. Pliny the Elder (AD 23–79), the Roman writer and administrator, remarked that when the Nodus Herculanus, otherwise the reef or square knot, was used to bind wounds, they healed much quicker, and first aid instructors today still insist on the reef knot being used for bandages and slings, although they are generally unaware of the knot's ancient origins.

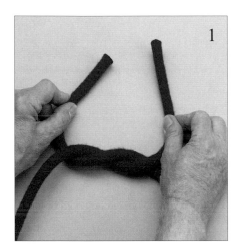

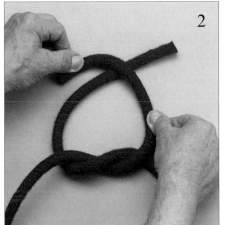

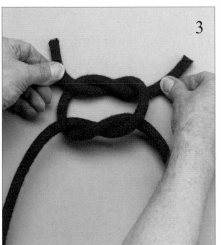

1 Tie a half-knot with both working ends.

2, 3 Add a second half-knot, which must be of opposite handedness to the first. In other words, if the first one was left-handed or S-laid, as illustrated here, then the second must be right-handed or Z-laid.

4 Tighten the knot.

REEF-KNOT LOOP

Incorporate this knot into a lifeline for a neat clip-on loop, or make one in a rope waist-tie. and slip a hammer, spanner, hand-axe or other tool into it.

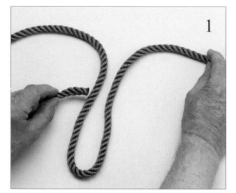

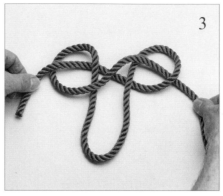

1 In the standing part of the line, form a closed loop or bight.

2 Bring the left-hand working end across in front of both loop legs, but locate it behind the other w'end.

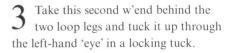

3 Take this second w'end behind the two loop legs and tuck it up through the left-hand 'eye' in a locking tuck.

4 Now bring the right-hand w'end back across the front of both loop legs and behind the left-hand w'end.

5 Take that w'end back behind the two loop legs and tuck it up through them to complete the knot as shown.

6 Tighten.

WEST COUNTRY WHIPPING

This is not the neatest of whippings that can be used to prevent the cut end of a rope from fraying and unravelling, but it is a robust one.

BOATING & SAILING

HOUSE & GARDEN

1 With a short length of whipping twine, tie a half-knot (either S-laid or Z-laid) around the rope to be whipped.

2 Take both working ends around to the back of the rope and add a second half-knot of the same handedness.

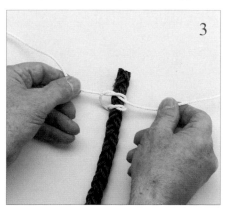

3 Bring the w'ends around to the front again and tie an identical third half-knot.

4 Continue this process until the whipping is at least as long as the rope is thick.

5 Finish off with a reef knot.

SURGEON'S KNOT

This binding knot, tied in both ends of the same lace or lashing, is more secure than a reef knot. It is used by surgeons to tie off the ends of blood vessels.

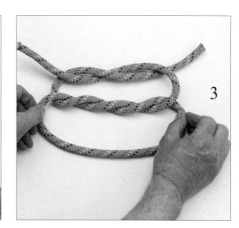

1 Tie a half-knot.

2 Make a second tuck with the working end.

3 Add a second half-knot of opposite handedness. In other words, if the first one was left-handed/S-laid (as illustrated), then the second must be right-handed/Z-laid.

4 Tighten, allowing both short ends to relocate themselves on opposite sides of the knot.

ROUND TURN & TWO HALF HITCHES

This strong yet simple knot, which can be tied almost in the time it takes to say its name, will check the momentum of a moving boat or other weight or load, and then secure it.

3 Add a half hitch.

4 Add a second half hitch.

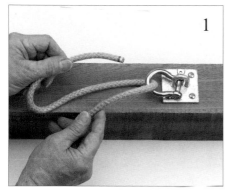

1

3

4

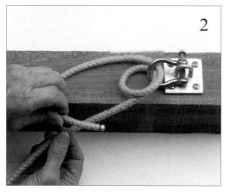

2

5

1 Pass the working end of the line through a ring (as illustrated), or around a rail, post or spar.

2 Tuck the w'end once more to form a round turn and use the friction generated to control any load upon the standing part.

5 Pull the resulting knot snug and tight.

ANCHOR BEND

This knot is believed by some to be rather stronger and somewhat more secure than the round turn & two half hitches already described.

The name of this variant of the round turn & two half hitches originated when it was used to bend a rope to the ring of an anchor where, being submerged, wet and likely to become slimy, it would have needed extra nip and grip.

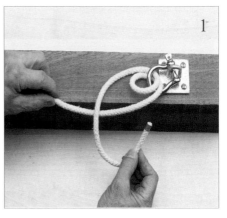

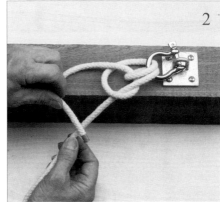

3 Add a second half hitch.

4 Pull the knot snug and tight.

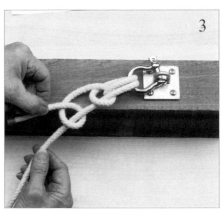

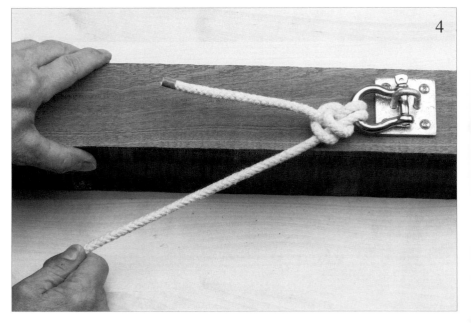

1 Take a round turn through a ring, or around a rail, post or spar.

2 Tuck the working end through the round turn and then tie a half hitch.

BUNTLINE HITCH

This simple but secure hitch is in effect two half hitches, the second trapped within the first, and deserves to be better known. Use it for flag halyards and any other cordage attachment that is likely to be shaken loose.

A buntline hitch was used aboard sailing ships to brail up square-sails, which flapped and flogged and were more likely to shake a less secure knot undone. When tied in a flat material, it is actually the common necktie knot, known by dress-conscious wearers as the 'four-in-hand'.

1 Tuck the working end through the ring, or other point of attachment, then lead it in a figure of eight around the standing part as shown.

2 Next, bring the w'end, from right to left, behind or under the standing part and up through in front of the other knot part.

3 Finally, tuck the w'end through to form the second half hitch. Leave a draw-loop for easy untying later.

4 Alternatively, pull the w'end completely through and tighten the knot.

BOATING & SAILING

HOUSE & GARDEN

OUTDOOR PURSUITS

BRACELET BINDING

This is a neat knot with which to embellish any cylindrical gift-wrapped parcel.

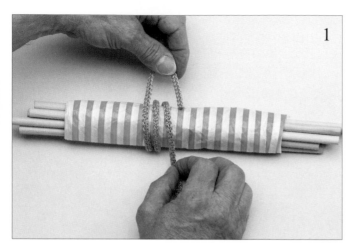

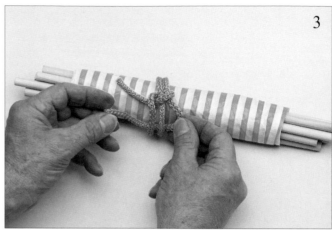

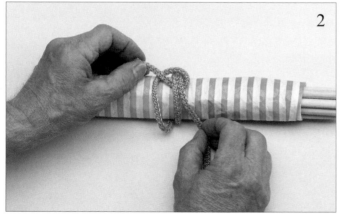

1 Wrap a short lace or lashing twice around the item to be tied up.

2 With the upward pointing w'end, tie a half hitch around the remaining two parts of the round turn.

3 With the other w'end, tie a second half hitch around two knot parts.

4 Dress and tighten this knot so that it takes on a neat diamond shape.

HALF-HITCHING

Use this technique to tie up long, cylindrical parcels, such as a roll of carpet, a sail lowered in harbour, or DIY plastic sheeting, bought from a hardware store or garden centre.

1 Tie an overhand loop in one end of the lashing and tuck the other end through it to form a running noose. Use this as the first part of the binding.

2 Then form an underhand loop and pass it over the end of the parcel to create an encircling half hitch.

3 Maintaining tension, make a similar third half hitch, and as many more as are required, to contain the length of the object being secured.

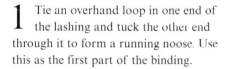

4,5 Turning the corner, return with the working end, tying a 'crossing knot' around the first of the encircling cords as illustrated.

6 Repeat this process at each crossing point.

7 Finish off with a couple of half hitches.

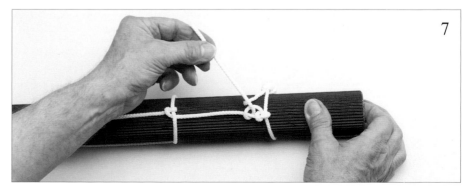

MARLINE-HITCHING

At first glance, marline-hitching would appear to be identical to half-hitching. Do not be deceived. It is different, as half-hitching is tied in the bight. Slide it off its foundation and it will fall apart. Marline-hitching, on the other hand, is tied with an end. Remove it and a string of overhand knots will be the result. Marline-hitching holds more securely during the tying process and so may be more appropriate when securing, say, a roll of plastic floor covering, that tends to unroll itself very easily.

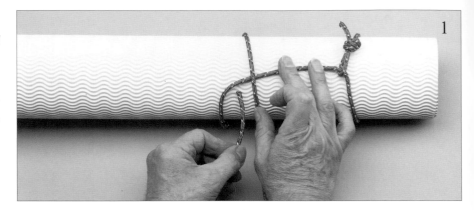

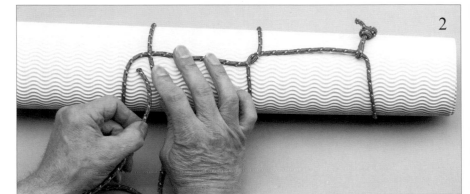

1 Start with a running noose (see half-hitching).

2 Tie a half-knot with the w'end to form the interlocking 'elbows' that are the basis of this binding. Repeat as often as necessary.

3 Finish off with a series of crossing knots and a couple of half hitches (see half-hitching).

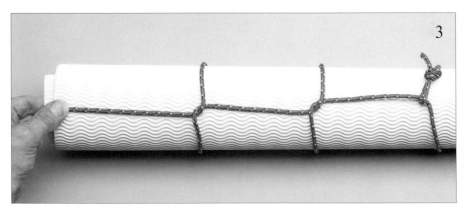

WHAT KNOT?

HANDCUFF KNOT

This knot may never have been used to immobilize prisoners. In fact it is more likely to have been used to hobble horses and pack animals overnight, so that they could graze but not stray far before daylight came. Who knows? Anyway, it is a fun knot to tie and its decorative appearance makes it a natural for curtain tie-backs. To finish off, cut, tease and comb both loose ends to form tassels.

3,4 Pull the left-hand leg of the right-hand loop down and out through the left-hand loop. At the same time pull the right-hand leg of the left-hand loop up and out through the right-hand loop.

5 Adjust both loops to the required size and tighten the completed knot.

HOUSE & GARDEN

OUTDOOR PURSUITS

CAVING & CLIMBING

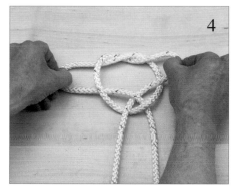

1 Working from right to left, form a couple of overhand loops.

2 Overlap them, right over left, as shown.

SHEEPSHANK

This is a handy method of shortening a rope that is too good or too costly to cut. It is also the basis of a bell-ringers knot and the trucker's hitch (page 178).

1 From right to left, form a series of three overhand loops, with the middle one somewhat bigger than the others.

2 Partially overlap the loops – right on top of middle, middle on top of left – then pull the left-hand leg of the middle loop down though the left-hand loop, at the same time pulling the right-hand leg of the middle loop up through the right-hand loop.

3 Arrange the completed knot as shown.

4,5 To secure this knot, rendering it semi-permanent, simply pull a standing part completely through the adjacent loop.

6 Alternatively, lay the loop on its nearby standing part and clip a shackle or karabiner through, over-under-over, to lock one to the other.

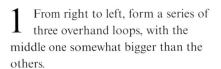

64

FIREMAN'S CHAIR KNOT or TOM FOOL'S KNOT

This is a time-honoured method of rescuing by lowering an ill, injured or otherwise helpless person from a blazing building, a cliff-top or over the side of a ship. The patient may be seated (as the name of the knot implies) or lying on a stretcher. One loop is fitted around the armpits and chest, the other around the back of the thighs. The knot can also be adapted to raise or lower a person from within the confines of a vertical shaft. As someone above pays out – or hauls in – one part of the rope, another below holds the other part to steady the patient and keep them clear of obstructions. Although factory-made and inspected webbing harnesses are preferable, there may come a time when one is not to hand, which is when self-sufficiency comes in useful.

The earliest reference to this rescue knot came from the Victorian fire chief, Eyre Massey-Shaw, in 1876. Scouting manuals usually quote the similar handcuff knot be used for this purpose, but fire services do not agree and prefer to use the superior Tom Fool's knot, which they consider to be easier, quicker and potentially less troublesome.

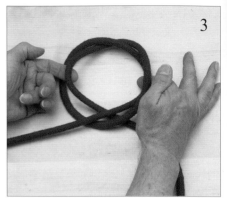

1 From right to left, make a couple of overhand loops.

2 Overlap the loops, left on top of right.

3 Pull the left-hand leg of the right-hand loop up through the left-hand loop, at the same time, pulling the right-hand leg of the left-hand loop down through the right-hand loop.

4 The knot to emerge has the same number of crossing points as the handcuff knot (page 63) but is in fact the subtly different Tom Fool's knot. Adjust each loop to the required size and tighten the knot.

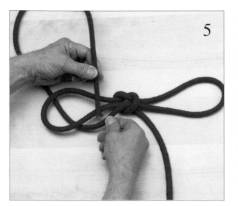

5 Lock the right-hand loop by tying a half hitch with its standing part around the left-hand loop.

6,7 Then lock the left-hand loop by tying a half hitch with its standing part around the right-hand loop.

8 Pull and tighten both half hitches snugly alongside the central Tom Fool's knot.

CHAPTER TWO
FIGURE-of-EIGHT KNOTS

'There is actually very little that can go wrong when tying the figure of eight, but people sometimes end up with … a figure of sixteen or even thirty-two!'

from Nigel Shepherd's
The Complete Guide to Rope Techniques, 1990

There is a consensus among knot-tyers that it is a good idea to get to know the common figure-of-eight knot, and its more sophisticated relatives, as soon as possible. This is because the various members of this clan are in regular use, not only as stopper knots, but they can also assume the roles of more than one bend or hitch and several loops, both fixed and sliding. Incidentally, an older name for the figure-of-eight knot, still to be seen in some knotting manuals, is the Flemish knot.

Climbers and cavers, whose lives literally depend on the knots they use, prefer figure-of-eights because they are easy to remember and simple to tie, even when they themselves are cold, wet, fatigued and frightened. Team leaders, when checking for safety, also like the unmistakable feel and easily recognized layout of the knots, which makes their job that much easier to perform.

Tie a basic figure-of-eight knot loosely in the middle of a short length of cord, then either run one of your hands along it, so as to overturn it, like turning a glove or sock inside-out, and the result will be a mirror-image of the original knot. Stop halfway and you have a knot that resembles a pretzel – a salty biscuit traditionally baked in the form of a knot. Knot theorists call this action 'flyping' (rhyming with 'typing') and it is an elementary exercise in the study of knot symmetry or handedness. Reverse the flype and the original knot reappears.

FIGURE-of-EIGHT KNOT

As a stopper knot in cord and rope, this knot is preferable to the simple overhand or thumb knot because it is more easily untied after use.

1 Make an overhand loop.

2 Give it a half-twist by lifting the left-hand side of the loop over to the right-hand side.

3 Then begin to pull the working end up through the larger loop. Stop at this stage, if you like, and leave a draw-loop for quick release later on.

4,5 Otherwise, pull the w'end completely through the knot and tighten it so that the end is pulled over at an angle to the standing part of the line.

Purely out of scientific interest, because there is no immediate practical application, try 'flyping' the knot as already outlined in the introduction to this section.

WHAT KNOT?

STEVEDORE KNOT

This makes a bulkier stopper knot than the figure-of-eight, and is more easily untied after use.

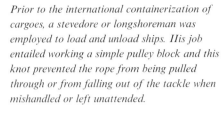

Prior to the international containerization of cargoes, a stevedore or longshoreman was employed to load and unload ships. His job entailed working a simple pulley block and this knot prevented the rope from being pulled through or from falling out of the tackle when mishandled or left unattended.

1 Make an overhand loop.

2 Give it a half-twist, as if to tie a figure-of-eight knot.

3 Then add two more half-twists.

4 Finally tuck the working end up through the largest loop and tighten the resulting knot.

FIGURE-OF-EIGHT KNOTS

FLEMISH BEND

This is a strong and reliable bend for two ropes or cords, although it can be tough to untie once it has been heavily loaded.

TIP *Arrange the two knotted cords or ropes so that, unlike parallel railway lines, they swap sides each time they change direction at the ends of the knot. This results in a neater knot.*

1 In one working end, tie a figure-of-eight knot.

2 Introduce the second w'end into this knot so that it lies alongside the first w'end.

3 Then follow the original lead around and through the knot to duplicate it.

4,5 Tighten the doubled knot, taking care to eliminate ugly and unwanted twists.

FIGURE-of-EIGHT BEND

This is an alternative to the Flemish bend, best suited for larger ropes, and easier to untie after use.

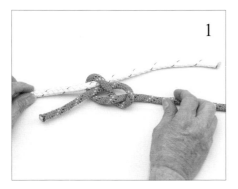

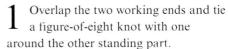

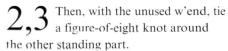

1 Overlap the two working ends and tie a figure-of-eight knot with one around the other standing part.

2,3 Then, with the unused w'end, tie a figure-of-eight knot around the other standing part.

4 Tighten both knots and pull on the standing parts to bring them together.

BOATING & SAILING

HOUSE & GARDEN

OUTDOOR PURSUITS

FIGURE-of-EIGHT HITCH

This simple hitch works best on rings, posts, rails or spars that have a much larger diameter than the cord or rope used. The hitch must be carefully arranged in order to be secure, but it is quick and easy to tie and desirable for these reasons. Simpler can be better.

1 Pass the working end over the anchorage point.

2 Bring the w'end across, from right to left, in front of the standing part; then take it, from left to right, around behind.

3 Next tuck the w'end through to complete the figure-of-eight layout.

4 Finally, work the knot snug and tight beneath its foundation.

FIGURE-of-EIGHT NOOSE

The adaptability of the figure-of-eight layout is further demonstrated by this adjustable loop, which can even be used to form a temporary 'hard eye', i.e. one where a thimble is inserted. Although a scaffold knot (pages 128–129) makes a longer-lasting loop, this figure-of-eight version is more easily untied after use.

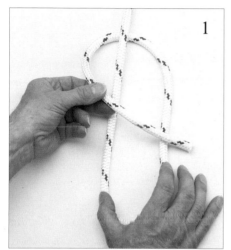

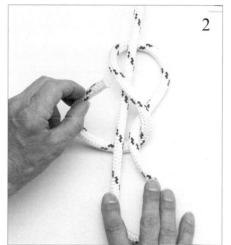

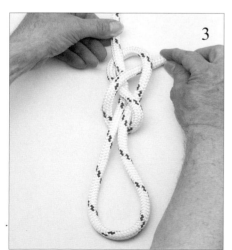

1 Make an underhand loop and bring the working end, from left to right, across in front of both loop legs.

2 Then pass the w'end, from right to left, behind both loop legs.

3 Next tuck the w'end down through the top right opening.

4 Finally, tighten the knot.

FIGURE-OF-EIGHT KNOTS

FIGURE-of-EIGHT LOOP

A strong and secure all-purpose fixed single loop, this can be tied in all kinds of cordage, thick or thin. It is noticeably easier to untie after use than the more basic overhand loop.

1 With a longish bight or closed loop in the end of the line, form an overhand loop.

2 Give it a half-twist by lifting the lower part of the loop over the upper part.

3,4,5 Bring the end of the loop or bight around and tuck it, from right to left, up through the loop.

6 Dress, and begin to tighten the completed knot, removing undesirable twists.

7 Tighten the knot.

TIP See Flemish bend (page 72).

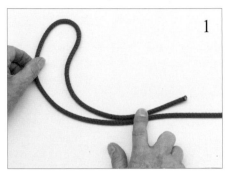

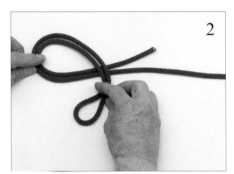

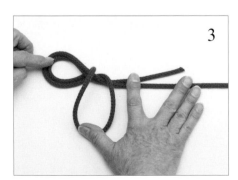

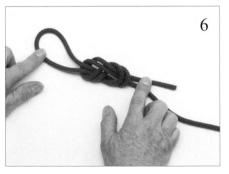

BOATING & SAILING

OUTDOOR PURSUITS

CAVING & CLIMBING

DOUBLE FIGURE-of-EIGHT LOOPS

With a method of tying similar to that of the bowline in the bight (page 88), this alternative twin-loop knot can be used as an emergency chair knot (see also fireman's chair knot, pages 66–67), when no properly tested and certificated harness is readily available. But it will more routinely serve as a hitch around two close but separate anchorages.

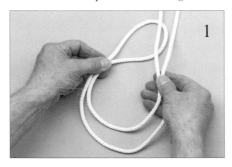

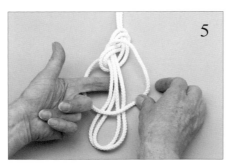

1,2 Use a long bight of line to begin a figure-of-eight.

3,4 Pull a section of the bight up and out through the lower loop (as shown) to form the twin loops that characterize this knot.

5 Bring the working end of the initial bight down in front of the existing knot, then pluck the twin loops up and through it.

6 Take the bight back up behind the knot to lie beside the doubled standing part.

7 Dress and tighten the completed knot.

BOATING & SAILING

OUTDOOR PURSUITS

CAVING & CLIMBING

TRIPLE FIGURE-of-EIGHT LOOPS

Using a tying method similar to that of the triple bowline (page 90), this alternative loop knot can be an emergency chair knot (see also fireman's chair knot), when no properly tested and certificated harness is readily available. But it will more routinely serve as a hitch around three close but separate anchorages.

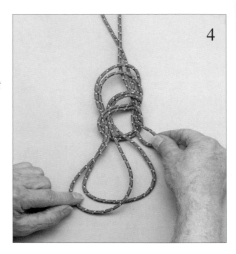

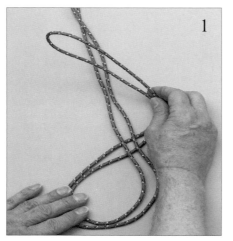

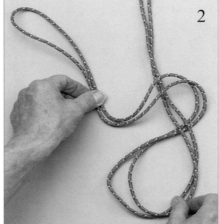

1,2,3 Begin as if tying the double figure-of-eight loops previously described.

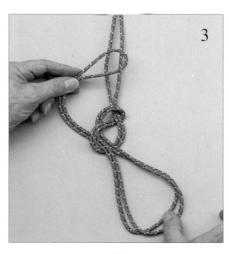

4 Pass the working bight, from left to right, around in front of the double standing parts, then down to tuck up through the twin loops already created.

5 Dress and tighten the completed knot.

FIGURE-of-EIGHT COIL

Use this coiling method to tidy any sizeable length of rope that is to be stored or put away.

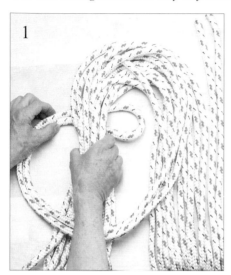

1

2

3

1 Locate the centre of the rope, put both ends together, and coil it doubled. Then separate the middle bight and bring it around the front of the coil in a clockwise circle, as illustrated.

2 Next pass the bight, from left to right, around behind the coil.

3 Tuck the bight through, over itself, from front to back of the coil.

4 Tidy the arrangement and the coil is ready to be hung up.

4

Chapter Three
Bowlines
& Sheet Bends

'The bowline is the King of Knots, because it is strong, secure, and versatile, as kings should be. And simple, as kings generally are.'

from Brion Toss's
The Riggers Apprentice, 1984

The layouts of the bowline and the sheet bend are more or less identical – an instance of the Parsimony Principle – although their w'ends and st'ends are deployed in different ways. The word bowline ('boh-linn') is short for 'bow line knot', which was tied aboard square-rigged ships and led forward, that is towards the bows, to help keep the weather edge of a sail tight and steady when beating into the wind.

When knot-tyers say the bowline is the King of Knots, they are not necessarily reporting their own experiences and opinions, but merely repeating something they have picked up, with no idea how it originated.

It is, in fact, a line from a mid-20th-century poem in praise of the bowline by A.P. (Sir Alan Patrick) Herbert, the English author, playwright, librettist and reformist activist, who certainly knew his knots.

Stone Age peoples used the sheet bend as a 'mesh knot' in fishing nets, and it has also been used since the earliest days to mend broken threads in the warp and weft of weaving looms, which is why yet another name for it is the ' weaver's knot'.

Knots are best learned on a one-to-one basis, from someone who knows how to put them across. Don't worry if you have difficulty following a knot's contruction from a diagram on a printed page – everyone does at first. If at first you don't succeed, tie, tie and tie again.

BOATING & SAILING

HOUSE & GARDEN

OUTDOOR PURSUITS

BOWLINE

The common bowline is a classic fixed loop, the favourite of yachtsmen and women, because it holds fast when needed but can easily be let go. Despite its soubriquet 'the King of Knots', however, it is not all that strong or secure. Nevertheless it has survived the transition from natural fibre to synthetic cordage and remains part of every knot-tyer's repertoire, both afloat and ashore.

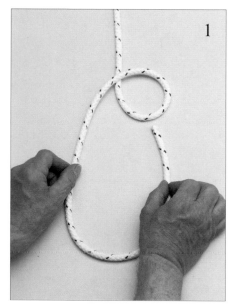

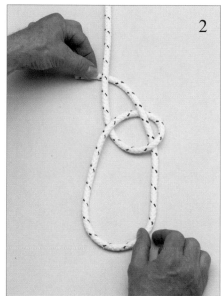

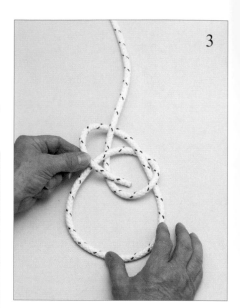

1 Make a small overhand loop and bring the working end around as shown.

2 Pass the w'end up through the loop, from back to front, and then from right to left behind the standing part of the cord or rope.

3 Then tuck the w'end down through the loop.

4 Tighten.

TIP Leave the w'end as long as the final loop. For added safety, if a secure knot is more important than a quickly untied one, affix the w'end to the nearest loop leg with tape or a double-overhand knot.

WHAT KNOT?

TWIN BOWLINE BEND

Use this cordage arrangement to join two large ropes of similar size and construction.

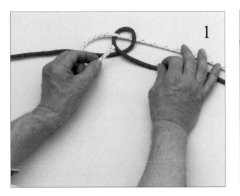

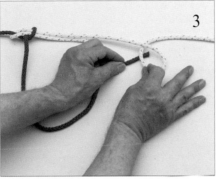

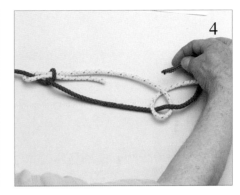

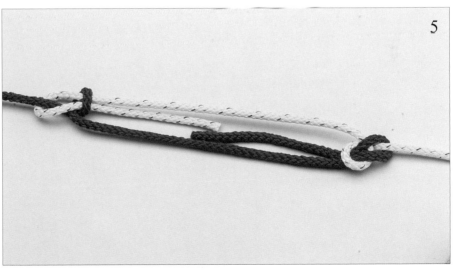

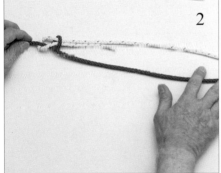

3,4 Repeat this process with the other w'end and standing part.

5 Tighten both knots so that there is an even strain upon both sections of the line between the two knots.

1 Overlap the two lines with their working ends pointing in opposite directions.

2 Make a small overhand loop in the standing part of one and pass the other w'end up and around and down through to tie a bowline, as shown.

83

WATER BOWLINE

When a bowline has to be towed through water, or dragged over rough terrain, this version of it is less likely to loosen and come undone.

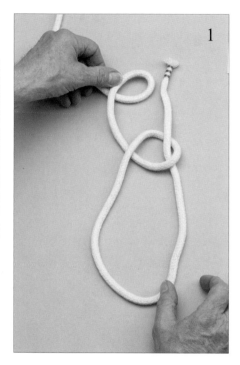

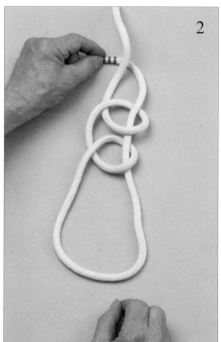

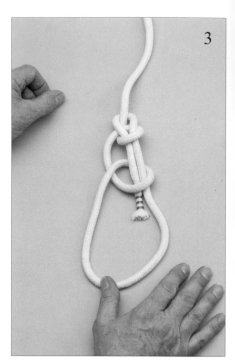

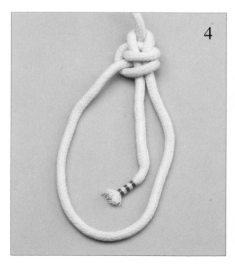

1 In the standing part of the line, form a couple of overhand loops.

2 Pass the working end up through both of them.

3 Take the w'end around behind the standing part of the line and tuck it down through each small loop in turn.

4 Tighten first the bowline itself, then the lower half hitch, which should fit snugly beneath the knot.

84

ROUND-TURN BOWLINE

As the common bowline is identical in layout to the simple sheet bend, but not in the way it is applied, so this version resembles the double sheet bend.

This knot is sometimes referred to as 'the double bowline', which is misleading, being only a single loop.

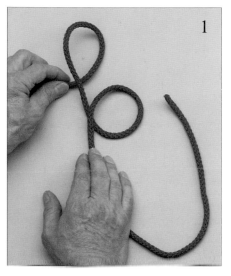

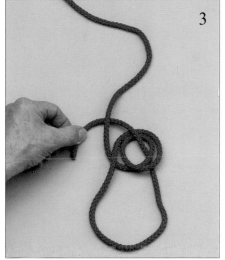

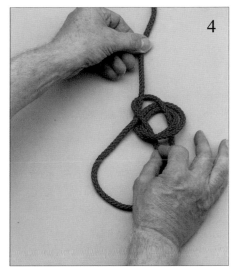

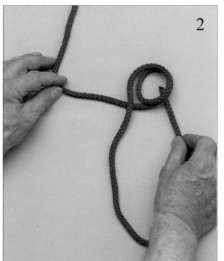

1 Make two overhand loops in the standing part of the line.

2 Overlap them to form a round turn and pass the working end up through it.

3 Take the w'end around behind the standing part.

4 Then tuck it back down through the round turn.

5 Tighten the resulting knot.

INUIT BOWLINE

This fixed loop is more compact and therefore a little more stable and secure than the common bowline. Its other name is the Boas bowline, after the U.S. anthropologist Franz Boas, who recorded its used by the Inuits of Baffin Island and Hudson Bay in 1907.

Inuit is the preferred term for an Eskimo of North America and Greenland, as distinguished from one from Asia and the Aleutian Islands, which is why this knot is understandably but mistakenly also called the 'Eskimo bowline'.

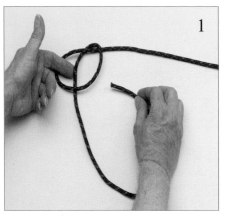

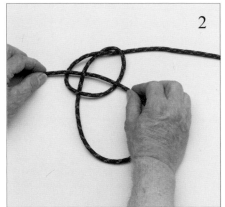

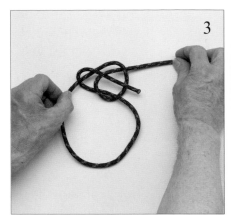

1 Make an overhand loop and bring the working end down behind it to outline a false overhand knot.

2 Tuck the w'end through – over/under/over – from right to left, as shown.

3 Then pull the standing part of the line and the left-hand loop leg apart, so that the knot capsizes into its final form.

4 Tighten.

LEFT–HANDED BOWLINE

A left-handed bowline is one in which the working end lies outside the loop instead of within it. It is debatable whether this is a good, bad or unimportant feature, and experts waver between them. The consensus seems to be that the left-handed bowline is unorthodox, though this is one useful application of the knot as a hitch to an anchorage point that is, or will at some time, be out of reach.

TIP While tying with a w'end is always preferable, a rope is rarely so long that it is impossible to pull the st'end through a knot as just described. This is not the way it is usually done, but it is allowed.

1 Contrive to pass a long bight of line through the ring or over the rail, post or spar that is to be the point of attachment.

2 Make an overhand loop in the standing part of the line.

3,4 Tuck the end of the bight up through the loop.

5 Then pull the standing end of the line through the bight to complete a left-handed bowline.

6 Tighten the knot, leaving the remains of the w'end within the ring or over the rail, post or spar.

Bowlines & Sheet Bends

BOWLINE (in the bight)

This is another of the so-called 'chair' knots, which can be improvised to hoist or lower an ill or injured person, with one loop under the individual's seat and the other around the chest beneath the armpits. A proper stretcher or harness is always preferable, and more comfortable, but there may be circumstances when only a knot like this will do. Then again, it is a useful hitch for two close but separate belaying points.

BOATING & SAILING

OUTDOOR PURSUITS

CAVING & CLIMBING

3 Pull the bight down in front of the two large loops and lift them, from behind, up and through to the front of the bight.

4,5 Lift the bight up and relocate it behind the standing parts of the knot. Tighten.

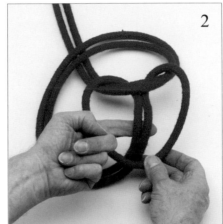

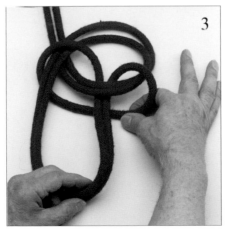

1 Double a longish bight in the end of the rope.

2 Make a small overhand loop in the doubled portion of line and pass the end of the bight up through it.

TIP The doubled sections of line within the knot ought not to be left lying, like railway tracks, parallel to one another. Instead, for the neatest finish, encourage them to swap sides once or twice as they turn and cross over themselves.

FRENCH BOWLINE

This is yet another chair knot from the days of mercantile and naval sailing ships. Nowadays, it makes a self-equalizing belay, as one loop can feed into the other, around a pair of anchorage points.

1,2 Make a small overhand loop. Lead the working end in a circle to form a larger loop.

3 Then take the w'end around once more to add a second large loop.

4 Next tuck the w'end up through the loops, as shown, and take it behind the standing part of the rope.

5,6 Finally, tuck it down to complete the familiar bowline layout. Tighten.

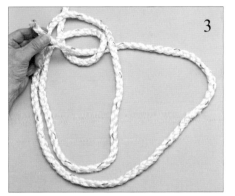

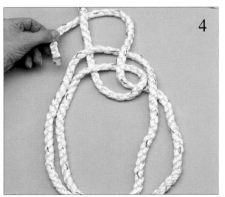

Some knots are named after the place where they originated, or the nationality of those who first used them. Another name for this knot is the Portuguese bowline.

TRIPLE BOWLINE

When improvising chair knots, it may be less uncomfortable to have two loops, rather than one, beneath the subject's seat, qnd the triple bowline achieves this. It will also belay to a trio of anchorage points, or lift and lower all kinds of routine and emergency equipment.

This is one of those knots that had us all saying, 'Well, of course. Why didn't I think of that?' It was demonstrated by the accomplished Canadian climber, Robert Chisnall, a past president of the International Guild of Knot Tyers.

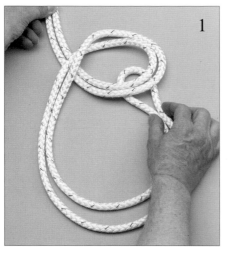

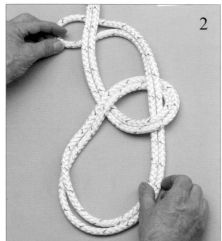

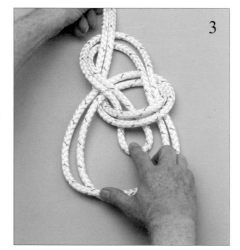

1 Double a long bight in the end of the rope.

2 Start to tie a bowline, but with the doubled section of line.

3 Tuck the bight end down through the existing two large loops.

4 Dress and tighten the resulting knot.

WHAT KNOT?

SHEET BEND

This is a classic, tried-and-trusted knot, with origins that lie deep in the past. Use it to unite two pieces of cordage that may be of dissimilar, but not too dissimilar, diameters and constructions.

Tip Locate both short ends on the same side of the knot because there is some evidence that, in some cordage, it may be less secure with the ends on opposite sides. Leave a draw-loop, if you like, for easier untying.

1 Bend the thicker or stiffer rope or cord into a short bight or closed loop.

2 Tuck the working end of the other cord or rope up through this bight.

3 Then lead this w'end around the short end of the other line and beneath the standing part.

4 Finally, bring it back on top to trap it beneath itself.

BOATING & SAILING

HOUSE & GARDEN

OUTDOOR PURSUITS

DOUBLE SHEET BEND

If the common sheet bend is tied with one cord or rope, that is very much thicker
or stiffer than the other, it may capsize and spill. Try this more secure version.

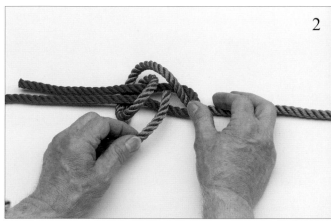

1 First tie the basic sheet bend.

2 Then lead the working end around a second time and trap it beneath itself.

3 Ensure both wrapping turns lie snugly side by side, and tighten the knot.

ONE-WAY SHEET BEND

If the knot has to be pulled through a narrow gap, or dragged over an uneven surface, it may be helpful to use this streamlined version.

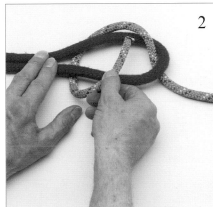

1,2 Tie a basic sheet bend.

3 Turn the working end around and tuck it back through itself, in a figure of eight, to lie alongside the other w'end and standing part.

4 Tighten.

THREE-WAY SHEET BEND

When three separate lines converge on a single point, try tying them together with this easy and effective knot.

This arrangement was spotted by the Swedish yachtsman, artist and magazine columnist, Frank Rosenow, on the town quay of Gaio in Antipaxos, Greece. He illustrated it in 1990 in his book, Seagoing Knots.

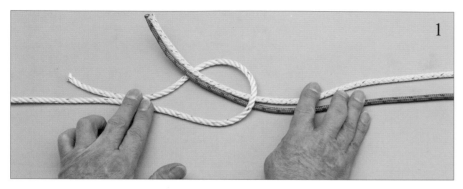

1 Make a bight or closed loop in whichever is the main rope or cord.

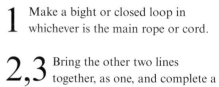

2,3 Bring the other two lines together, as one, and complete a sheet bend.

4 Tighten.

LAPP KNOT

Use instead of a double reef bow to do up a dressing-gown cord, as a curtain tie-back, or as an improvised safety lifeline or tether.

1 With one end, form a short bight or closed loop, and lay the other working end diagonally across the top of it as shown.

2 Next, pass the w'end behind both legs of the bight.

3 Then make a small overhand loop in the w'end, tucking this over itself and down through the initial bight.

4 Begin to tighten the completed knot.

5,6 Arrange it so that the w'end is trapped between the resulting three-part crown.

TIP Draw-loops should be used more often. Not only do they make knots easier to untie, they may also actually strengthen them by adding an extra section within the heart of a knot and so reducing sharp curves and nips. Although not all draw-loops produce a perfect quick-release, because there may still be layers of a knot to be picked apart, the Lapp knot does fall apart without further ado when the w'end is tugged and the draw-loop withdrawn.

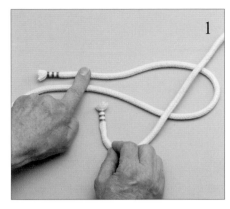

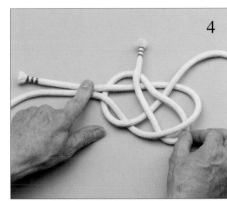

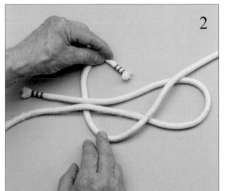

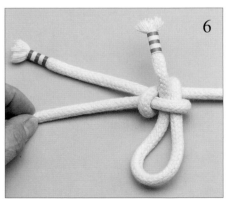

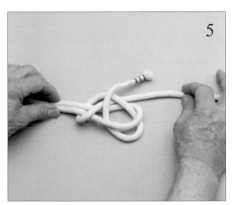

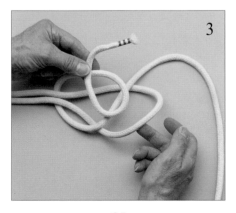

SIMPLE SIMON (1)

This derivative of the sheet bend is slowly becoming better known, and deservedly so.

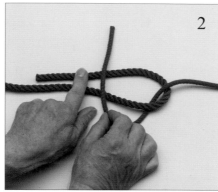

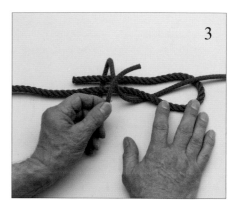

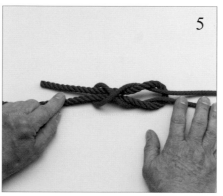

1,2 Make a short bight or closed loop in one of the cords or ropes.

3,4 Tuck the other working end down, through the bight, then lead it up and around both bight legs as shown.

5 Next pass it diagonally over itself before tucking it up through the bight beside its own standing part.

6 Tighten.

SIMPLE SIMON (2)

This alternative to the previous knot takes a fraction of a second longer to tie,
but is a little more secure.

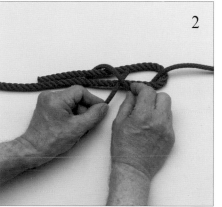

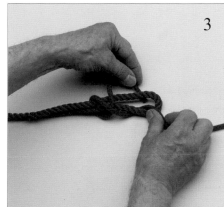

1 Make a short bight or closed loop in one cord or rope, and tuck the other working end down through the bight before wrapping it (as shown) around both bight legs.

2 Next pass the w'end beneath itself.

3 Then tuck it up through the bight so that it emerges alongside its own standing part.

4 Tighten.

Both of these Simple Simon bends were devised by the late Dr. Harry Asher, and first appeared in his, A New System of Knotting – Volume 1, published in 1986 by the International Guild of Knot Tyers.

HEAVING-LINE BEND

A rope or cable that must reach across an intervening gap, or up to a high point, is generally hoisted into position by means of a much lighter 'messenger' or heaving line, that has been thrown up or over ahead of it. The knot that attaches one to the other is the heaving-line bend.

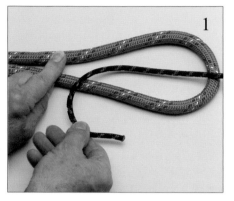

3 Then bring it back across the front of the bight …

4 … and tuck it beneath itself as shown.

5 Tighten this arrangement.

1 Make a bight or closed loop in the larger rope or cable and lay the thinner line on top of it.

2 Take the working end around behind the bight or loop.

RACKING BEND

Try this, for a more robust variation on the heaving-line bend.

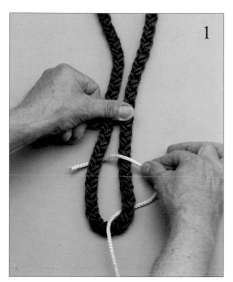

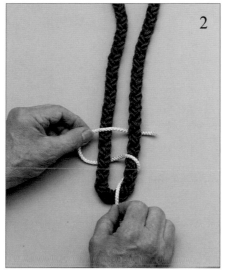

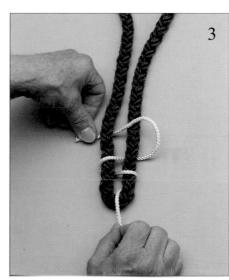

1 Make a longer bight or closed loop in the rope or cable, and introduce the working end of the heaving line, as shown.

2 Begin to interweave the w'end in a series of figure-of-eight tucks and turns.

3 Continue these 'racking' turns as often as necessary to keep the thicker bight or loop together.

4 Lastly, trap the w'end beneath its final turn.

5 Tighten as necessary.

SEIZING BEND

This less fiddly alternative to the racking bend is also more readily untied after use and may be preferable for that reason.

This original bend is another innovation from the fertile fingers of knotting researcher, Dr. Harry Asher. It first appeared in Issue number 29, October 1989, of Knotting Matters, the quarterly magazine of the International Guild of Knot Tyers.

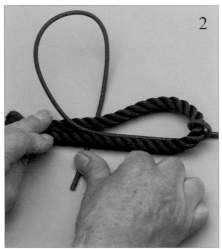

1 Make a bight or closed loop in the rope or cable, then insert the other working end beneath this bight. Lead it in a backwards circle and tuck it once more up through the bight.

2 Lay the w'end along the standing part of the bight, then begin to wrap it around both legs of the bight.

3,4,5 Continue to wrap firmly, each turn placed neatly alongside the previous one, until the w'end reaches the end of the bight, as shown.

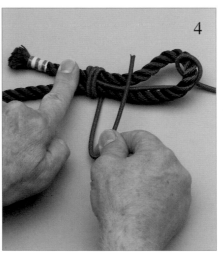

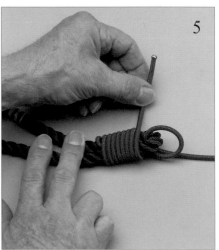

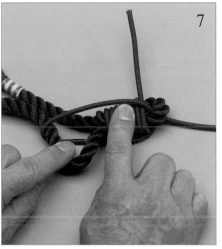

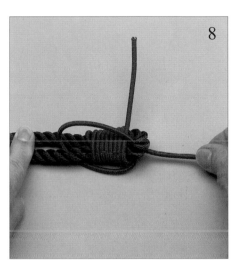

6 Now pull out the initial round turn made around the bight with the w'end.

7 Insert this long loop between the two bight legs to create what is known as a 'frapping' turn, that runs the length of the other wrapping turns.

8 Pull the standing part of the thinner line so as to reduce the frapping turn.

9 Finally tighten the frapping turn so that it holds its own w'end trapped in place.

CHAPTER FOUR
CROSSING KNOTS

'In the dictionaries, the Clove Hitch is sometimes called the Builder's Knot …the builder himself is probably unaware that he has a knot named for him.'

from Clifford W. Ashley's
The Ashley Book of Knots, 1944

A feature of the knots in this section is that they all have one or more parts lying diagonally, pressing down upon and securing other underlying turns. This is a recipe for excellent hitches and superb bindings, which include the constrictor (single and double), the frustrator, and the boa (belt-and-braces in one knot). Many of these knots can also be tied slickly and quickly in the bight instead of with an end.

Once more, you will recognize the usefulness of grouping knots according to form rather than function, as you discover the similarity between the scaffold hitch and the pole lashing, the rolling hitch and the midshipman's hitch.

The is evidence to suggest that the jug, jar or bottle sling was known to the ancient Greeks and Romans, who may have used it to lift and manhandle the heavy amphorae containing wine and oil, or even as a surgical sling or traction device for dislocated joints.

There is no short cut to learning any of the knots in this section, or other sections of the book, but neither is it compulsory to tackle them all. You can cherry-pick. Turn the pages, and when you see a knot you like, have a go. You don't even have to learn a simpler one first. Sometimes, tying a more complicated knot makes learning the simpler ones easier still.
Knotting ventured, knotting gained.

CLOVE HITCH (tied with an end)

Use this quick and easy hitch to tie up a small boat, or as part of a more elaborate mooring scheme for a larger craft. Then again, utilize it to suspend objects from lanyards. The clove hitch is almost certainly identical to the knot the ancient Greeks called Nautikos brokhos (nautical noose), which they also used as a simple surgical sling, or traction device for a broken limb or dislocated joint, and to secure splints.

1 Pass the working end through a ring, or around a rail or spar, then bring the w'end in front of its own standing part and lead it diagonally upwards (in this instance, from right to left).

2 Pass the w'end through or around the belaying point once again.

3 Lastly, tuck the w'end up beneath its diagonal section to outline a letter N (or its mirror image), and work the knot snug and tight.

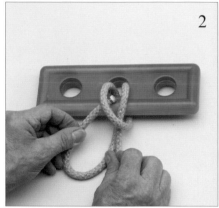

TIP Sometimes a clove hitch can jam, for instance, in wet and swollen cordage made from natural fibre, or after it has been heavily loaded, when it may be difficult to untie. So consider using a draw-loop for the final tuck.

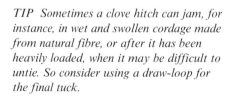

WHAT KNOT?

CLOVE HITCH (tied in the bight)

When the knot can be slipped over a post, or onto the end of a rail or spar, it is quicker and easier to tie it in the bight.

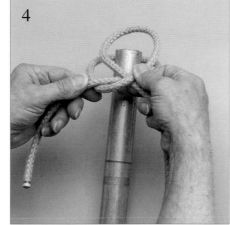

BOATING & SAILING

HOUSE & GARDEN

OUTDOOR PURSUITS

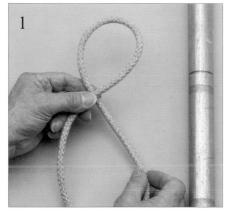

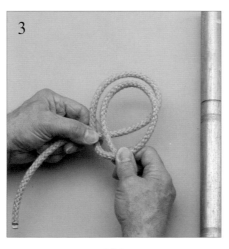

1 Form an overhand loop.

2 To the left of it, make a second overhand loop.

3 Overlap them, right over left.

4 Slip this couple of loops onto the anchorage point.

5 Work the resulting knot so that it is snug and tight.

SCAFFOLD HITCH

There was once an era, less safety-conscious and litigious than today, when men went aloft to work high up on seats improvised from a scaffold plank and a couple of hitches. No longer is this regarded as best industrial practice, but the technique is a nifty one all the same, and could still be useful on rare occasions.

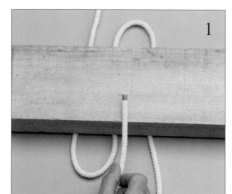

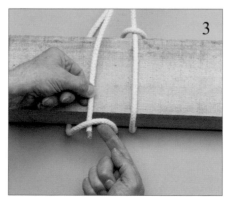

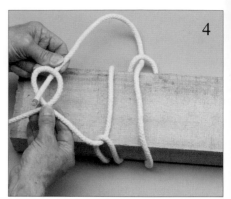

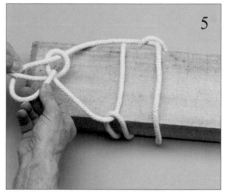

1,2 Lay out a length of line in a S-shape beneath the plank, then tuck one working end over and through the bight opposite it.

3 Tuck the other w'end through the other bight.

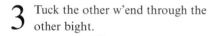

4,5 Form an underhand loop in the standing part of the line, then use the w'end to tie a bowline.

6 Pull the arrangement taut, so that both bights and legs of the bowline are loaded evenly. Tie a second knot (not illustrated) at the other end of the plank.

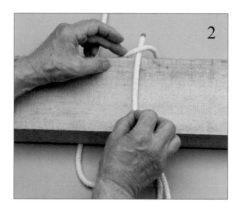

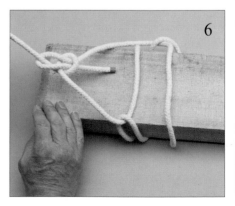

As the U.S. rigger and author Brion Toss remarks in The Rigger's Locker (1992), 'Old knots never die; they just wait for us to come to our senses.'

WHAT KNOT?

POLE LASHING

By first tying the scaffold hitch, previously described and illustrated, you can then easily adapt it to collect together what might otherwise be an awkward armful of garden tools or other disparate bits and pieces.

4 Add a second half-knot (of opposite-handedness) to complete a reef knot.

5 Repeat this at the other end to produce a pair of pole lashings.

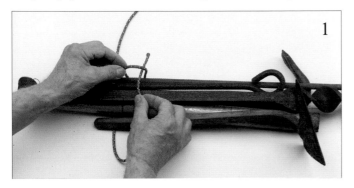

1

3

2

4

1 Lay a lace or lashing in an S-shape beneath one end of the items to be collected together.

2 Tuck each working end through its opposite bight.

3 Pull the arrangement that results up tight and tie a half-knot.

5

107

ROLLING HITCH

Use this hitch to attach a line to a rail, post or spar, when the pull will occur at an angle other than a right angle.

TIP The pull must come on the side of the knot that has the two diagonal turns against the standing part.

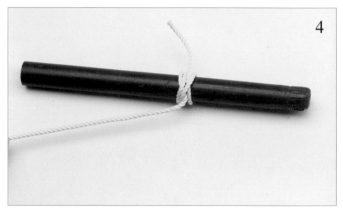

1 Pass the working end over and around the belaying point.

2 Lead it diagonally upwards (from left to right in this instance) to cross over and trap its own standing part, then take it down behind the foundation again.

3 Make a second diagonal pass, snugly alongside and to the right of the first one. Then lead the w'end down behind the foundation once more, this time to emerge on the right-hand side of the standing part. Tuck it up beneath itself.

4 Tighten the knot.

MIDSHIPMAN'S HITCH

Unlike many other loops, which are either fixed or sliding nooses, this is an adjustable, slide-and-grip loop. Tied like the rolling hitch (opposite), the size of the loop can be altered by sliding the knot along in the hand; but, once loaded, it creates a dog's leg deformation in the standing part of the line, so that the knot tends to hold fast wherever it is.

1 Make an overhand loop and bring the working end up through it from back to front.

2 Lead the w'end up and over the standing part in a diagonal wrapping turn.

3 Take a second similar turn with the w'end, placing it snugly beside and, in this instance, to the left of the first one.

4 Lead the w'end around the standing part once more, then tuck it beneath itself.

5 Tighten the knot.

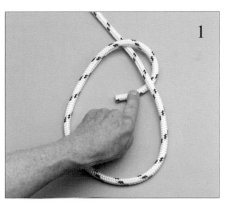

TIP If your life should ever depend upon hanging onto a rope thrown to you by a rescuer – and there is no other alternative – you could do worse than pass the line around beneath your armpits before tying this knot.

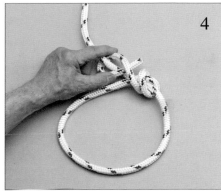

CONSTRICTOR KNOT (tied with an end)

This is arguably the world's best simple yet semi-permanent seizing. It is tied in seconds and will grip like the boa constrictor after which it is named. Use it, with or without a draw-loop, as first aid on the cut ends of cordage, to keep a hosepipe on a tap, to hold together carpentry components while glue dries, or for any number of uses that may suggest themselves. Indeed, this may have been the 'gunner's knot' used to seize the necks of flannel-bag gunpowder cartridges for muzzle-loading artillery.

TIP To remove a constrictor, without marking and scarring the foundation within, merely sever the overriding diagonal knot part with a sharp knife, when the knot will fall away in two curly segments.

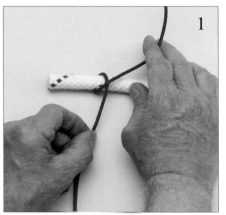

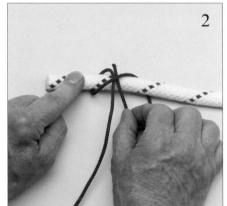

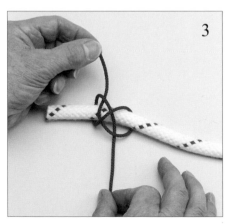

1,2 Tie a clove hitch (see page 104).

3 Then tie a half-knot (in this instance left-handed or S-laid) in the parallel working end and standing part.

4 Tighten.

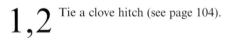

CONSTRICTOR KNOT (tied in the bight)

This super little knot can be tied more quickly in the bight.

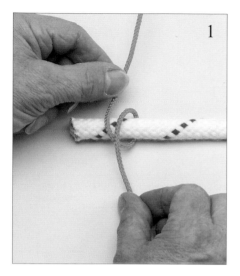

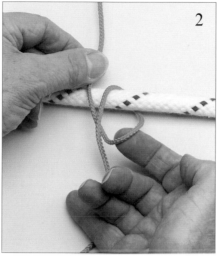

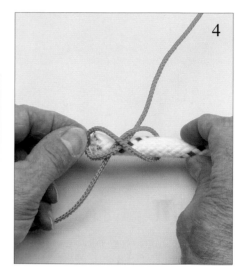

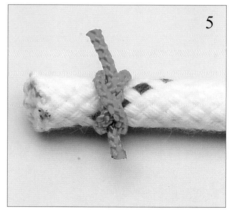

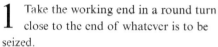

 Take the working end in a round turn close to the end of whatever is to be seized.

2 With finger and thumb, pull out a bight or loop from the lower part of the round turn, to the side of the standing part furthest fron the end of the foundation.

3,4 Give a half-twist to it (in this instance, counter-clockwise), and place the bight or loop over the end of the rope foundation.

5 Tighten.

TIP Whether tied with an end or in the bight, it is sometimes enough to pull this knot hand-tight, though you can, in tough materials, lever both ends tighter still, using a couple of marlinspikes or other handy tools as improvised handles. For neatness, cut and trim the ends as close to the knot as you like – the constrictor will not come undone.

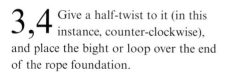

House & Garden · Outdoor Pursuits

DOUBLE CONSTRICTOR
(tied with an end)

Sometimes a single constrictor may be a little less reliable – for example, if the cordage in which it is to be tied is too thin, or the item to be seized is too thick – when a double constrictor knot will remedy any shortcomings.

1 Pass the working end around, then up and across itself (in this instance, from right to left).

2,3 Take a similar second diagonal turn, locating it snugly beside and to the right of the first one.

4 Next tuck the w'end up beneath both diagonals to lie alongside its standing part.

5 Tuck the w'end around the standing part to tie a half-knot.

6 Tighten.

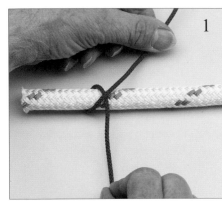

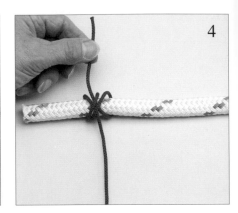

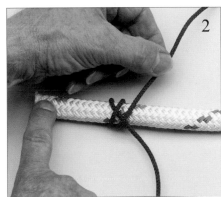

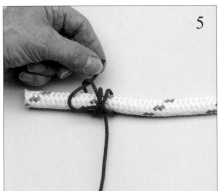

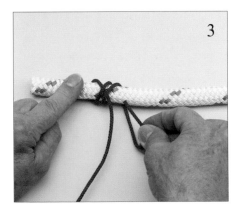

DOUBLE CONSTRICTOR (tied in the bight)

Once familiar with the single constrictor, this method of tying the double version will prove a simple matter.

This method of tying a double constrictor knot in the bight first appeared in Knots (1990) by U.S. rigger Brion Toss.

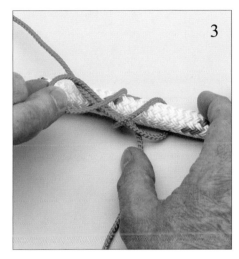

1 Tie a clove hitch, with the diagonal from bottom left to top right.

2 Pull the working end over to the left-hand side of the knot.

3 Next lift up a bight from the standing part, giving it a clockwise half-twist.

4 Then place the resulting loop over the end of whatever is to be seized.

5 Tighten.

CROSSING KNOTS

FRUSTRATOR KNOT

A binding akin to the constrictor, this firm little knot actively resists attempts to undo it, hence its name. Learn to tie it in the bight.

This knot was devised by the late Dr. Harry Asher, the uncle, incidentally, of the English actress and writer Jane Asher. The knot first appeared in Dr. Asher's, A New System of Knotting, Volume 2, published in 1986 by the International Guild of Knot Tyers.

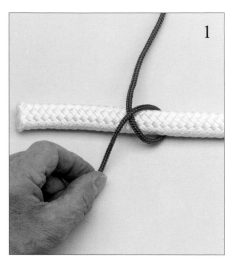

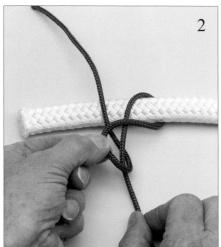

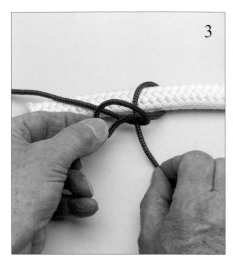

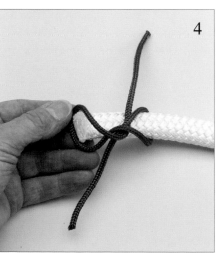

1, 2, 3 Begin as if tying a single constrictor in the bight (see page 111), taking a round turn with the working end, pulling out a bight or loop, and giving it a half-twist counter-clockwise.

4 Then give it a second half-twist, counter-clockwise, and place the resulting twisted loop over the end of whatever is to be seized.

5 Tighten.

TRANSOM KNOT

Use several of these binding knots to seize together a garden trellis of wooden lathes or bamboo sticks; to construct a Scout, Guide or Sea Ranger pioneering project; or as a useful 'third hand', when performing DIY tasks of any kind.

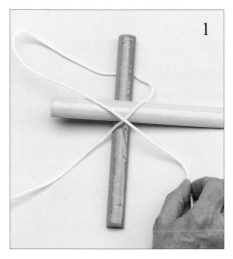

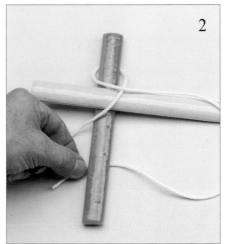

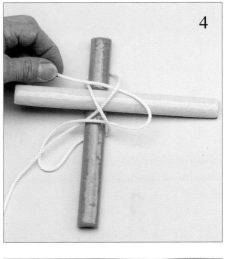

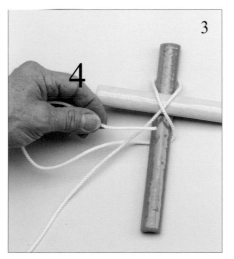

1 Take a short lace or lashing and lead the working end counter-clockwise around the upper vertical section to be seized, and then diagonally down, from left to right, over its standing part.

2,3 Pass it, from right to left, behind the lower section.

4 Finally, tuck the w'end – over, under, under (as shown) – to tie both w'end and standing part in a right-handed or Z-laid half-knot.

5 Tighten the resulting knot.

The well-known knotting author, Clifford Warren Ashley, wrote how he first used this knot to join the cross-pieces of his daughter's kite. The knot was closely related to the constrictor and, because of this, it is included in this section. In fact, remove both cross-pieces and it turns into a double overhand knot or strangle knot, and could justifiably have been featured in the first section of this book.

CROSSING KNOTS

BOA KNOT

This is a belt-and-braces of a binding, part double-constrictor, part-strangle knot. It is best tied in thin cordage, because too much friction between thicker component parts prevents it from tightening properly.

1 Place a short length of whipping twine on a flat surface in a loop, as shown.

2 Lay a second loop atop the first one.

3 Pick up the right-hand side, consisting of three parts, giving it a half-twist.

4 Replace it so as to create a figure of eight.

5 Insert the foundation to be seized, going under, over, under, as shown.

6 Tighten the resulting knot, taking care to eliminate needless twists and cross-overs.

The boa knot was rediscovered, named and promoted in 1996 by the weaver Peter Collingwood, who wanted a knot that would remain securely in place when the cluster of threads, around which it was tied, was cut and trimmed close to the knot. Others, it later transpired, had been using the knot before him, but then, this is often the way in knotting.

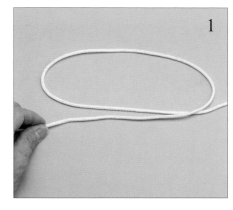

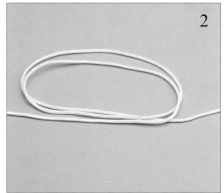

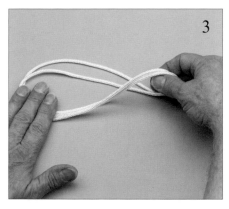

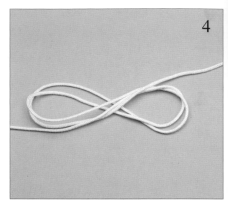

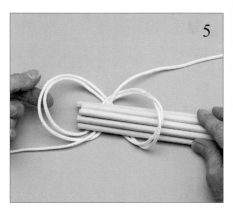

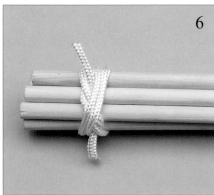

HOUSE & GARDEN

OUTDOOR PURSUITS

116

GROUND-LINE HITCH

Use this quick and simple hitch when a more secure belay than a clove hitch is required. It works well enough in round cordage, but could have been made for flat tape/webbing.

This knot has been used by both cod fishermen on their trawl nets, and by horse soldiers to tether their mounts to a picket line, so it certainly comes tried-and-tested.

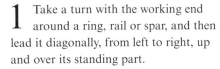

1 Take a turn with the working end around a ring, rail or spar, and then lead it diagonally, from left to right, up and over its standing part.

2 Lead the w'end down behind the anchorage, then forward.

3 Then pass the w'end diagonally up, from right to left, and tuck it beneath its standing part.

4 Tighten.

BOATING & SAILING

OUTDOOR PURSUITS

CAVING & CLIMBING

GROUND-LINE COIL

This is a neat and easy way to keep a coil tidy and tangle-free.

1 With a working end, make a half hitch around the coiled rope.

2 Take the w'end around the coil once more.

3 Then tuck it beneath itself as shown.

4 Tighten.

SNUGGLE HITCH

This strong and secure knot is more easily tied with an end, but because it collapses if slid from its foundation, it can be tied in the bight.

3 Take the w'end around and down behind the foundation once again, then diagonally up (from right to left once more) to go over, under, in a final locking tuck.

4 Tighten the knot.

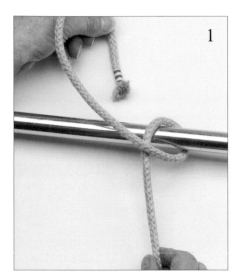

1 Take a turn with the working end around the belaying point, so that the w'end crosses diagonally, from left to right, up and over the standing part.

2 Lead it over and down behind the foundation, as shown, then bring it across, from left to right, in front of the standing part to tuck up beneath the diagonal knot part.

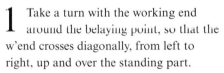

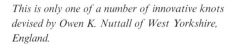

This is only one of a number of innovative knots devised by Owen K. Nuttall of West Yorkshire, England.

CROSSING KNOTS

DOUBLE FIGURE-OF-EIGHT BINDING

In terms of toughness, this robust binding lies somewhere between the constrictor, strangle knot and boa knot. Strictly speaking, it is tied in the bight, although to describe the process requires writing about ends.

This is another innovative hitch from Owen K. Nuttall, though it seems to make a first-rate binding knot, too.

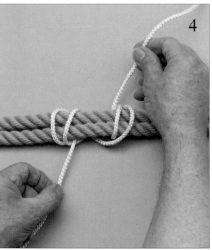

1 Lay out the lace or lashing in a symmetrical figure of eight as shown.

2 Lift up first one end, then the other, and lay each one in turn around on top of the nearest initial loop.

3 Then introduce whatever is to be seized, tucking under/over/under.

4 Start to tighten the knot by removing some of the slack.

5 Turn the work over and finish tightening the knot.

BOOM HITCH

This knot works well in round cordage, but beds down very satisfactorily in tape/webbing. Thrashing about in a stiff breeze on a spring ebb tide, in the estuary of the River Medway, in Kent, England, the mainsheet tackle of my 12-foot inflatable sailing dinghy suddenly broke free of the boom. With a short lanyard and this knot I re-attached it, which enabled me to beat back against wind and tide to the slipway, where my car and trailer were parked. Then, because it had proved to be at least as good as the failed aluminium rivets, I left the knot in place for the rest of that sailing season.

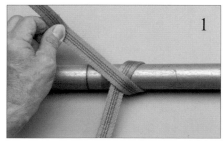

TIP Repeat to yourself, 'Wrap over, over, over, then tuck', while tying this knot.

1 Wrap the working end around the point of attachment as shown.

2 Lead the w'end up over the previously laid diagonal.

3 Then pass it down behind the foundation and bring it forward again to the right of the standing part.

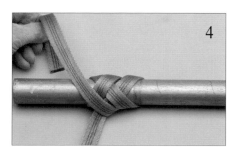

4 Lead it up once more in a second diagonal.

5 Then pass it down once more behind and around the foundation, to emerge at the front, and tuck up beneath itself.

6 Tighten.

BOTTLE SLING

This clever cord arrangement will grip tightly around the neck of a jug, jar or bottle of your favourite drink, so that it can be handily carried or immersed in a river or stream to keep it cool. It will also assist when lugging around heavier demijohns of water or, with suitable safeguards, hazardous chemicals.

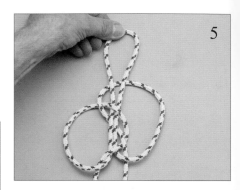

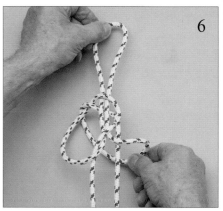

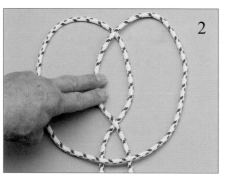

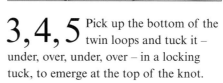

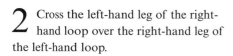

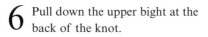

On the left margin (vertical tabs): BOATING & SAILING — HOUSE & GARDEN — OUTDOOR PURSUITS

1 Make a long bight or closed loop in a lace or lanyard and bring the top of it down to rest on the two standing parts as shown.

2 Cross the left-hand leg of the right-hand loop over the right-hand leg of the left-hand loop.

3, 4, 5 Pick up the bottom of the twin loops and tuck it – under, over, under, over – in a locking tuck, to emerge at the top of the knot.

6 Pull down the upper bight at the back of the knot.

7 Pull down the upper bight at the front of the knot.

8 Arrange the resulting knot in the form of bracelet, with a small loop at the top, and two standing parts of different lengths.

9 Fit the knot around the neck of the jug, jar or bottle, and carefully tighten it. Then tuck one of the standing ends through the knot's small loop and tie it to the other st'end with a fisherman's knot or a tape/webbing knot to create a self-equalizing pair of carrying handles.

There is evidence to suggest the knot was also known to the ancient Greeks and Romans, who used it as a surgical sling and for applying traction to broken or dislocated limbs.

CHAPTER FIVE
WRAP-AND-TUCK KNOTS

'What a good knot a Monkey's Fist is for a young beginner – nice and big, and not too difficult to make. And you can do all sorts of destructive things with it afterwards.'

Captain Allan McDowall in
Knotting Matters, Number 43, Summer 1993

This is a section not usually found in other knotting manuals. Why then are some of the knots, such as the scaffold knot or the double and triple fisherman's knots, not included with the overhand knots upon which they are based? Well, it is the method of tying them that singles them out. As soon as you become proficient at these more advanced versions, you will find yourself twirling and tucking w'ends in a way not possible with simpler knots. And so the wrap-and-tuck category creates itself.

Experiment with the law of loop, hitch and bight (already explained in the Introduction), to discover how some of the knots can be tied in the bight, including the angler's loop, the scaffold knot or noose and   surprisingly – Jack Ketch's noose, although it would be more trouble than it is worth to do so. Some of the simpler knots, such as the strangle knot, can only be tied with an end.

The corkscrew knots are undoubtedly the most innovative cordage contrivances in this section. The two methods illustrated and explained are only the first of a small clutch of other such knots devised by the French circus performer, Olivier Péron, who published a series of slim booklets describing them in 1998.

WRAP-AND-TUCK KNOTS

STRANGLE KNOT

This is an ugly name for a neat knot which, removed from whatever it is used to contain, turns out to be a double-overhand knot. The method of tying it, however, is what makes it suitable for this section.

The Swedish knotting expert, Hjalmar Öhrvall, in his book Om Knutar (1916), preferred this knot to the constrictor (pages 110–111) because its turns bedded down more snugly.

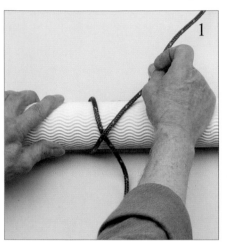

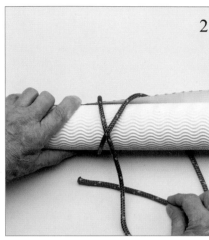

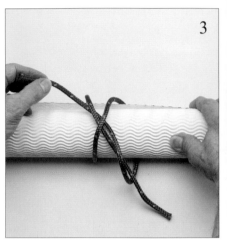

1 Wrap the working end around the intended cylindrical parcel or package, then bring it diagonally up, from left to right, across its standing part.

2 Pass the w'end, from right to left, behind the standing part.

3 Then lead the w'end back across the standing part, as if to tie a rolling hitch (see page 108), but turn it sharply to the left and tuck it – under/under – to complete the knot.

4 Leave a draw-loop for easy untying, if desired, and tighten the knot.

5 Otherwise, pull the w'end completely through and tighten.

WHAT KNOT?

ANGLER'S LOOP (tied in the bight)

There are times when this knot can only be tied with an end (see page 47).
Where possible, however, it is more slickly tied – almost, it seems, by sleight of
hand – in the bight.

1 With the working end, make an
underhand loop.

2 Then wrap the w'end up behind this
loop. Bring it down again in front of
the emerging knot …

3,4 … and pull the initial wrapping
turn, to the left, over/under to
form the actual fixed loop. Tighten.

This knot has been called 'a single bowline in the bight'.

SCAFFOLD KNOT

Use your knowledge of the triple-overhand knot to produce this sliding loop or noose.

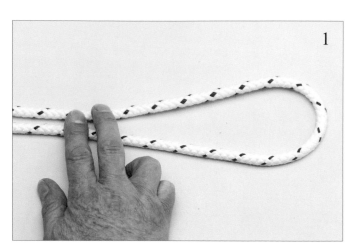

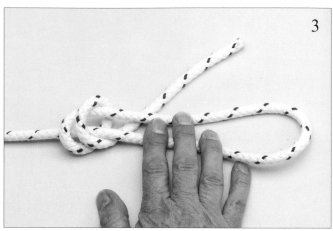

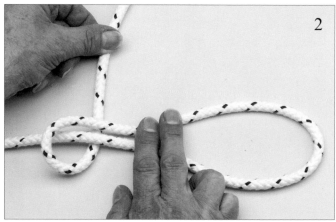

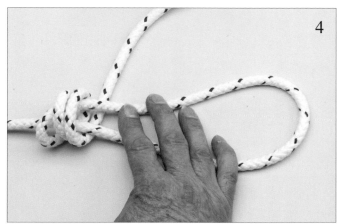

1 Make a bight or closed loop in one end of the cord or rope.

2 Wrap the working end down, around and up at the back.

3 Wrap the w'end down, around and up at the back again ...

4 ... and again.

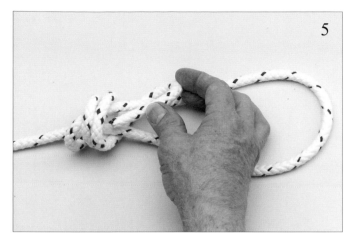

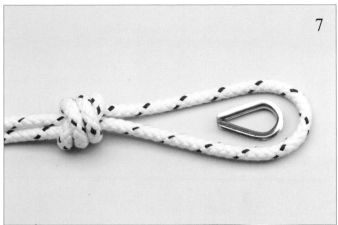

5 Bring the w'end down in front of both loop legs and tuck it through the trio of wrapping turns.

6 Tighten the knot.

7 To make a 'hard eye' (that is, one reinforced with a metal or plastic thimble), simply insert a thimble of the correct size for the cord or rope …

8 … and slide the knot up against it.

TIP Make the wrapping turns around a forefinger to preserve a space through which to tuck the w'end. This was not illustrated, as it would have over-complicated matters. To untie quickly, first remove any thimble, then grasp the knot and simply tug on the standing part, when it will fall apart (indicating, of course, that it could be tied in the bight).

DOUBLE FISHERMAN'S KNOT

This makes a stronger bend than the basic fisherman's knot (see page 49) in nylon monofilament fishing lines and most synthetic cordage.

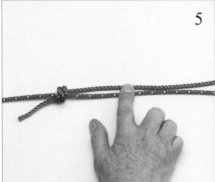

1 Lay the two lines to be joined alongside one another, with their working ends pointing in opposite directions.

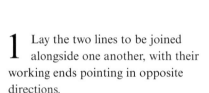

2,3,4 With one w'end, tie a double-overhand knot around the adjacent standing part.

5 Tighten this knot.

6 With the other w'end, tie another double-overhand knot (of identical handedness) around the other adjacent standing part.

Some climbers call this a 'grapevine' knot, while anglers, on the other hand, refer to it as a 'grinner' knot. For years it was assumed to be because of the 'smiley mouth' created between the twin knots before they slide shut, and it was not until Lee Bristow, of Williamsburg, Virginia, remarked that it could possibly be a corruption of the Anglo-Saxon word 'grin', meaning a snare for an animal, a trap, or a noose, that the true meaning possibly emerges.

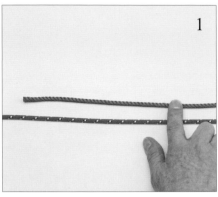

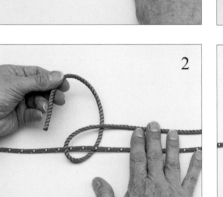

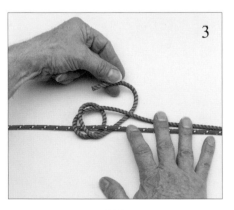

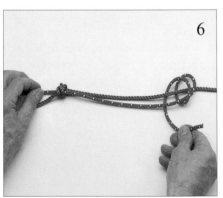

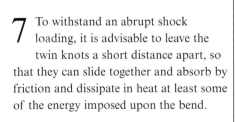

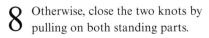

TRIPLE FISHERMAN'S KNOT

Bulky knots with many wrapping turns are generally stronger than skimpier versions of the same knot. Climbers and anglers like this knot: it takes a little longer to tie, and is more difficult to untie after it has been heavily loaded, but it can be relied upon to cope with heavy work.

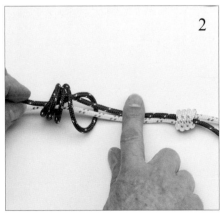

7 To withstand an abrupt shock loading, it is advisable to leave the twin knots a short distance apart, so that they can slide together and absorb by friction and dissipate in heat at least some of the energy imposed upon the bend.

8 Otherwise, close the two knots by pulling on both standing parts.

1 Place together the two lines to be joined, with their ends facing in opposite directions, and tie a triple-overhand knot with one working end around the adjacent standing part.

2 Tie an identical knot with the other w'end around the other standing part.

3 Tighten both knots and either leave them a short distance apart (not illustrated) or pull them together.

This knot is also known as a double grapevine or double grinner knot.

COMMON SEIZING

A seizing holds two sections of cordage side-by-side and is a mighty strong alternative to knotting or splicing. In this instance, it has been used to form an eye in a hawser.

1 Make a closed loop and bind the two legs together using a constrictor knot (page 110).

2, 3, 4 Begin to make a series of fairly tight wrapping turns, each located snugly alongside the previous one, until a distance of at least three times the diameter of the intended seizing has been covered.

5 Then bring the working end of the whipping twine up between the two legs of the loop.

What Knot?

TIP Use thinner whipping twine than the cord which, for added clarity, is shown in the illustrations.

6 Tuck it again down through the loop, around the back, and up between the loop legs. Repeat this once more to create two turns at right angles to the original wrapping turns. These act to tighten the entire seizing and are called 'frapping turns'.

7 Tuck the w'end down through the two frapping turns (from top to bottom of the illustration).

8 Then lead the w'end around (to the top of the illustration) and tuck it up through between the two frapping turns.

9 Pull the resulting loop knot (resembling one end of a reef knot) down between the two loop legs and trim off the two ends of twine.

133

WRAP-AND-TUCK KNOTS

BOATING & SAILING

OUTDOOR PURSUITS

CAVING & CLIMBING

HEAVING-LINE KNOT

When a heaving line or 'messenger' is thrown, the height and distance of its flight is often helped by the addition of a weighty knot on the rope's end. This is one such knot.

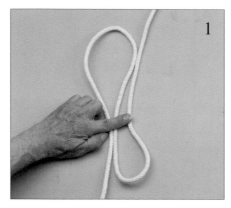

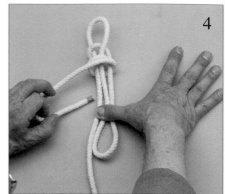

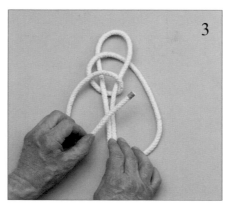

1 Fold or pleat the end of the rope into three parts.

2 Tuck the working end, from right to left – under/over – through the adjacent loop.

3 Next wrap the w'end, counter-clockwise, around the two loop legs.

4 Then wrap again, this time around all three knot parts, so as to draw them together into a triangular bunch.

5 Continue with more tight wrapping turns until the end of the lower bight is reached.

6 Tuck the w'end in a locking tuck, then remove unwanted slack to tighten the knot.

WHAT KNOT?

RACKING SEIZING

Figure-of-eight wrapping or 'racking' turns are the heart of this mighty strong seizing.

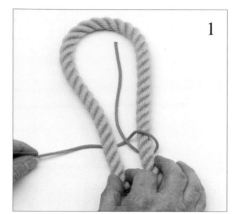

1 Make a bight or closed loop in the end of the rope to be seized, and arrange the whipping twine as shown.

2,3,4 Make a series of racking turns, leading towards the end of the bight or loop, in such a way as to enclose and trap the standing end of the twine.

5 Then wind the w'end downwards so that it lies between, and fills, the spaces between the racking turns.

6,7,8 Make two frapping turns as for a common seizing (see page 132), and secure the w'end with a seizing knot.

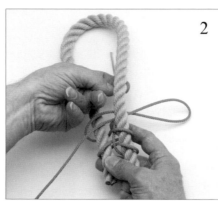

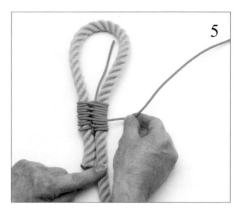

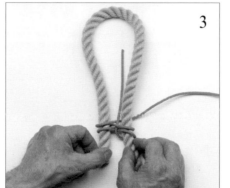

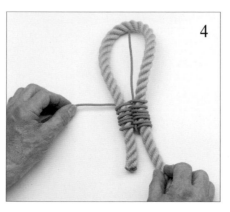

WRAP-AND-TUCK KNOTS

BLOOD KNOT

This is a classic angling knot. Its numerous wrapping turns make for a strong and secure knot in thin nylon fishing lines, but it works in round cordage, too.

TIP The two short ends are shown emerging on opposite sides from the knot. If, however, both ends emerge on the same side, and are left long, then they can be knotted together to form a useful mid-line loop.

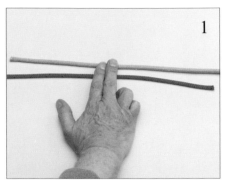

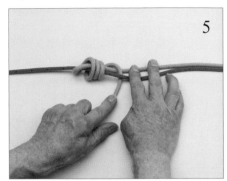

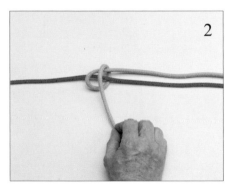

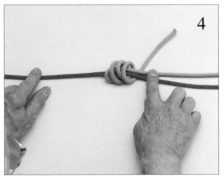

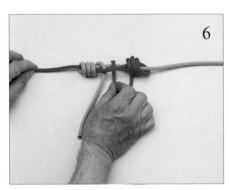

1 Lay the two lines parallel, ends facing in opposite directions.

2 Begin by wrapping one working end around the adjacent standing part and itself.

3, 4 Continue by wrapping three or four snug and tight turns.

5 Then tuck and trap the w'end between the two lines.

6 Repeat this process with the other w'end.

7 Pull the two sets of wrapping turns and trapped ends together.

136

COMMON WHIPPING

Rope-ends should be whipped, taped, or heat-sealed, either before or after they have been cut, to prevent them from fraying and unravelling.

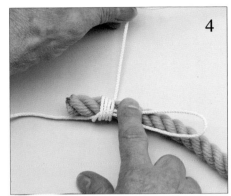

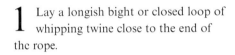

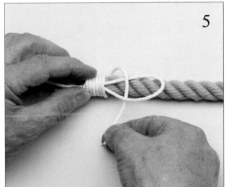

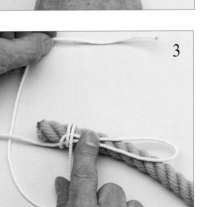

1 Lay a longish bight or closed loop of whipping twine close to the end of the rope.

2 Begin a series of snug and tight wrapping turns with the working end around the rope to trap this bight or loop.

3,4 Continue until these turns cover a length that is at least equal to the diameter of the rope.

5 Tuck the w'end down through the bight or loop.

6 Pull the unused end of the whipping until the bight or loop retreats beneath the wrapping turns, taking the w'end with it.

TIP Use thinner whipping twine than that which, for clarity, has been used here.

PERFECTED WHIPPING

The interlocking elbows, that lie beneath the wrapping turns of a common whipping, can produce an ugly bulge, and sometimes cause the twine to snap during tightening. This version overcomes both of these shortcomings.

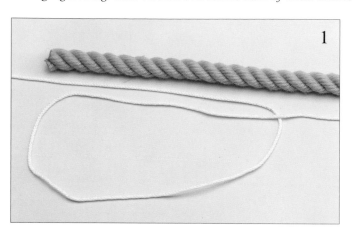

1 Make a large loop in a length of whipping twine.

2,3,4 Place it on the rope and begin a series of snug and tight wrapping turns, with the loop itself towards the rope's end.

138

5 Whenever necessary, untangle the left-hand standing end from the unused portion of the loop.

6,7 When the whipping has reached the required length (no less than the diameter of the rope), pull on the right-hand st'end to eliminate what remains of the loop.

8 Then pull on both st'ends to fully tighten the whipping.

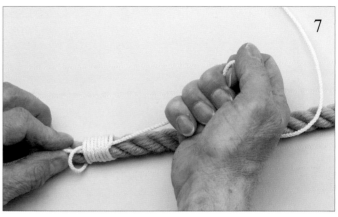

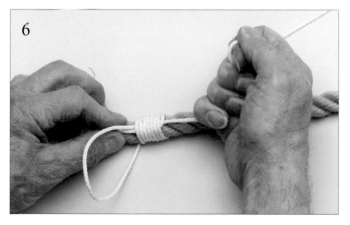

TIP During the wrapping, the loop will twist itself irremediably, and make tightening the whipping impossible unless something is done to prevent it from happening. So twiddle the right-hand trapped end (in this instance, up at the front, down at the back) to insert several deliberate twists into the working loop at the outset. Being of the opposite handedness to the ones the loop would make itself, they will disappear as the whipping builds.

SAILMAKER'S WHIPPING

This whipping is, in effect, stitched (although it does not require a needle) into a hawser-laid rope and retained there by three frapping turns that prevent it from slipping off.

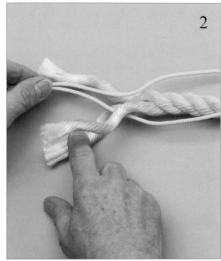

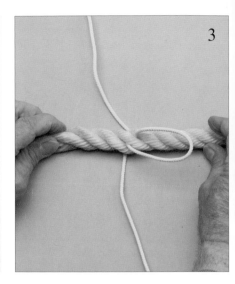

1 Unlay the three strands for a distance of several inches.

2 Make a long bight or closed loop in a length of whipping twine and place it over, one loop leg on each side of, the middle strand.

3 Re-lay the strands.

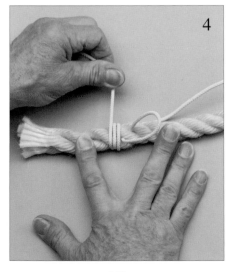

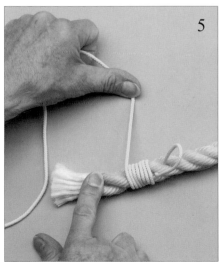

4,5 Make a series of snug and tight wrapping turns, towards the rope's end, leaving behind both the bight or loop and the standing end of the whipping twine.

6 Lift up the initial loop or bight and lay it along the rope, so that each one of its parallel legs follows one of the grooves located on either side of the strand that it surrounds, and then place it over the end of that strand.

7 Pull on the st'end to tighten the loop.

8 Then lay the st'end along the empty third groove.

9 Finally, tie both ends of the whipping twine together with a reef knot (see page 53) or a surgeon's knot (see page 56) and conceal it within the ends of the three strands.

TIP Use twine that is thinner than that which, for clarity, has been used here.

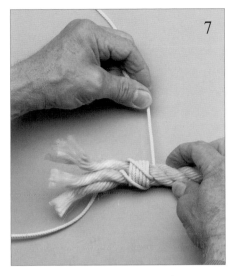

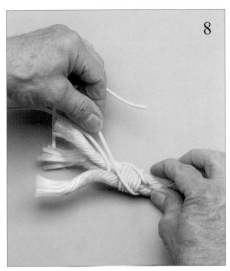

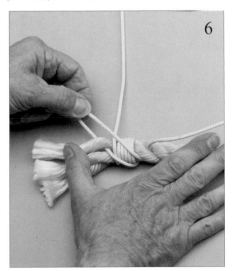

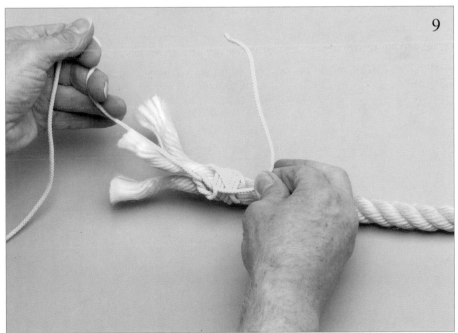

PALM & NEEDLE WHIPPING

The cut ends of braid-on-braid or sheath-and-core ropes, when not taped or heat-sealed, ought to be whipped.

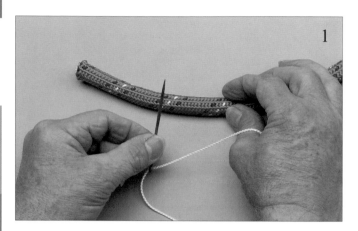

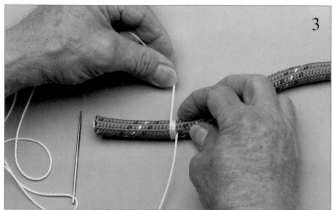

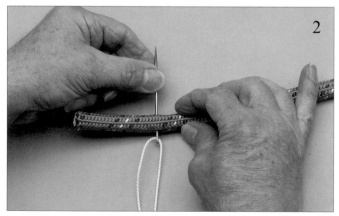

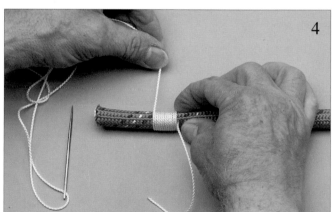

BOATING & SAILING

OUTDOOR PURSUITS

CAVING & CLIMBING

1,2 Pass the working end of the whipping twine through the rope.

3,4 Make a series of snug and tight wrapping turns, trapping the standing end of the twine, and covering a length at least equal to the diameter of the rope.

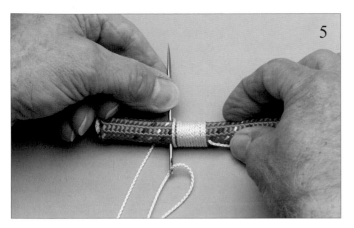

5,6 Stitch a couple of frapping turns along the length of the whipping.

7 Knot the w'end unobtrusively around the frapping turns.

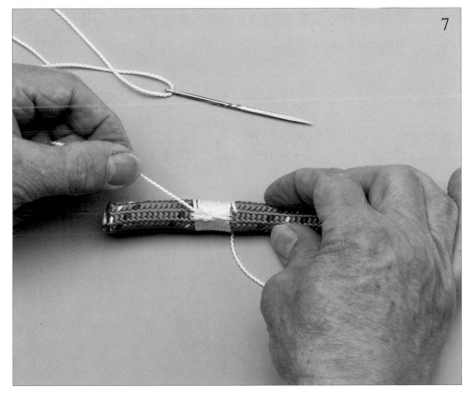

TIP Driving a needle through a hard-laid rope is best done wearing a sailmaker's palm; but soft-laid rope, as shown here, offers much less resistance and whipping twine can be safely stitched into it without the use of such protection.

JACK KETCH'S KNOT

This hangman's noose, despite its grisly connotations, makes a strong and useful general-purpose loop.

This knot is named after the 17th-century hangman, who was later lampooned in Punch and Judy shows.

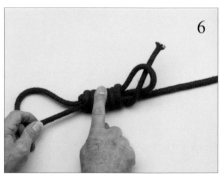

1 Fold or pleat the rope into three parts.

2,3,4 Make a series of snug and tight wrapping turns with the working end, so as to enclose the three rope parts in a triangular bunch.

5 Tuck the w'end through what will be the upper loop, as shown.

6 Pull whichever loop leg will close that loop.

7 Tightly trap the w'end and adjust the remaining loop to the required size.

SCOUT'S COIL

This compact hank will provide a come-in-handy length of cord to keep on your belt, using a knute hitch (see page 196), or in your grab-bag.

1 Tie a hangman's noose (opposite) with a long working end.

2 Tuck this w'end down through the loop.

3 Pull on the standing part of the rope to eliminate the loop …

4 … and so trap the w'end.

HOUSE & GARDEN

OUTDOOR PURSUITS

This neat device was used in the Boer War, in which Robert Baden-Powell made his name, which is probably why it later came to be associated with the Boy Scout movement he so famously founded. Once used by army scouts to keep their horses' leading ropes off the ground and out of harm's way, it also permitted them to quickly dismount and quietly lead their animals, when spying out the ground ahead of the troops.

CORKSCREW KNOT (1)

The discoverer of this knot claims that, for abseiling or rappelling on static or dynamic lines, it is superior to many other climbing knots, and that, because it will withstand shock loading of various intensities and differing frequencies, it is suited to acrobatic work, tree pruning, et cetera. It can be tied in the bight and released from a distance that is limited only by the doubled length of the rope.

This knot, and the one that follows, are just two of a family of such knots devised by the French circus performer, Olivier Péron, who published them in a series of booklets in 1998. Take care not to pull the draw-loop unless and until you wish to undo the knot. Note that the load will be on the short end.

1 Double the rope and loop the end over the belaying point.

2, 3, 4, 5 With what will be the loaded length of the line, make a series of snug and tight wrapping turns around the loop.

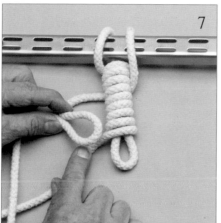

6,7 Lead the other end around the back of the wrapped loop and double it to form a bight or closed loop.

8,9 Tuck it through the remaining eye of the loop in the form of a locking tuck and draw-loop.

CORKSCREW KNOT (2)

Use this variation of the corkscrew knot, already illustrated and described on pages 146–147, to equalize the load between a couple of anchorage points.

4,5 Continue these wrapping turns until the loops are reduced to only a small eye.

6,7 Bring the other section of rope around into a bight or closed loop, then tuck it down through the eye as a locking tuck and draw-loop.

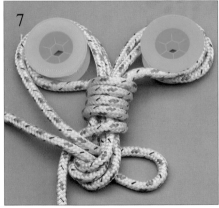

1 Double the rope and lay it over and around the two belaying points as shown.

2 Bring the right-hand loop across to join the two central loops.

3 With what will be the loaded end of the rope, begin a series of snug and tight wrapping turns that will enclose all six parts of the three loops.

148

WHAT KNOT?

ALPINE COIL

Here is another way to carry, transport or store a coil of rope and keep it tangle-free.

1 Bend the working end back alongside itself.

2,3,4 With the w'end, make a series of snug and tight wrapping tucks to enclose the initial bight or loop.

5 Tuck the w'end down through its own bight or loop.

6 Tighten.

149

MONKEY'S FIST

This handsome knot provides the weight that gives the extra height and distance to a thrown 'messenger' or heaving line.

BOATING & SAILING

HOUSE & GARDEN

OUTDOOR PURSUITS

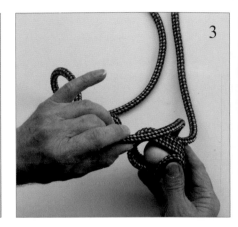

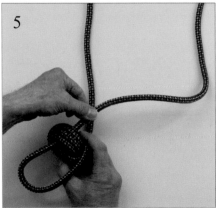

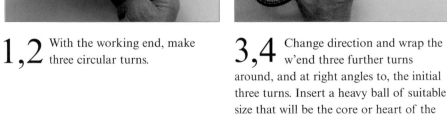

1,2 With the working end, make three circular turns.

3,4 Change direction and wrap the w'end three further turns around, and at right angles to, the initial three turns. Insert a heavy ball of suitable size that will be the core or heart of the knotted ball when it is completed.

5 Change direction once more and with the w'end begin to make a final three wrapping turns, this time at right angles to both the first and second set of turns.

WHAT KNOT?

6 Tuck the w'end over the second set of turns, but under the first set of turns whenever they are crossed.

7–10 Repeat this process until three locking turns have been completed.

11 Tighten the completed knot around its core or heart.

12 Tie the w'end to the standing part of the line with a suitable knot, in this instance, a water bowline.

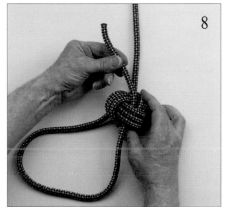

Chapter Six

MAVERICKS &
MUTATIONS

'Knots are like shape-shifters.

They can turn into other knots.'

Owen K. Nuttall
Knotting Matters, Number 90, March 2006

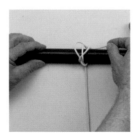

This is a pick-'n'-mix assortment of old and new, traditional and innovative knots, bends and hitches. Some, such as the harness bends (single and double), the farmer's loop, and the gaff topsail halyard bend, have survived unchanged for centuries to make the transition into modern cordage, while other vintage holdfasts, like the trucker's hitch (once the waggoner's hitch) and the Tarbuck knot, have been rejuvenated with a cosmetic nip-and-tuck. But there are a few more, such as the pedigree cow hitch, the versa tackle and the adjustable bend, that are relatively recent inventions or discoveries.

Whether or not new knots have been deliberately devised, or merely discovered, they can cause intense debate among knot-tyers. Some knots undoubtedly result from knowledge and skill purposefully applied to achieve a specific outcome (invention); others come about through fiddling fingers and curious minds (accident); then there is the serendipitous combination of turns and tucks that the prepared mind is quick to spot as an innovative piece of knotting (observation).

But it is never wise to say that any knot is new. For instance, in 1952, the British climbing writer, Ken Tarbuck, published an eponymous slide-and-grip loop to cope with the new-fangled nylon climbing ropes, unaware that it had been in use by tree surgeons in Wisconsin, U.S.A., since the 1940s or earlier. Then, as sheath-and-core (or kernmantel) construction gradually ousted hawser-laid stuff for climbers, the Tarbuck knot became redundant. Now, 50 years later, tests on a modified version may result to its rehabilitation as a life-support knot. This is how knotting goes.

CARRICK BEND

An old nautical knot for joining heavy cables or hawsers which, when pulled tight, would pass comfortably around a capstan.

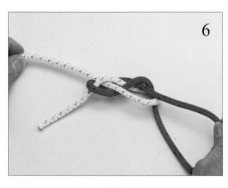

1 Make an overhand loop in the end of one of the ropes.

2 Lay the end of the other rope across it.

3 Take the second end under the standing part of the first rope.

4 Bring it back over the end of the first loop.

5,6 Weave the w'end under, over, under.

7 Haul taut.

To be pedantic, this is the Double Carrick Bend, but it is seldom referred to as such these days.

FALMOUTH CARRICK BEND

This tying method was devised by Owen K. Nuttall and appeared in Knotting Matters, Number 23, April 1988.

1 Make a bight in the end of one rope and lay a bight of the second rope across the first, keeping the working ends on the far side.

2 Take the w'end of the second rope under both branches of the first bight.

3 Bring the w'end up and out of the loop.

4,5 Lead the w'end of the first bight over three cords and under the fourth.

6 Carefully pull tight, keeping hold of the ends. The knot will spill over into a Carrick Bend.

Using either method, the ends come out on opposite sides, which is more secure than the heraldic, decorative version of the Carrick Bend, where both ends are on the same side.

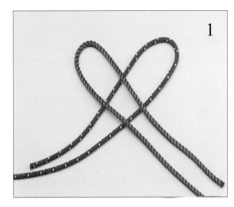

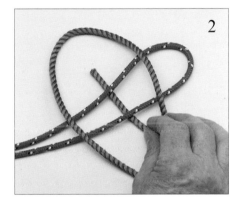

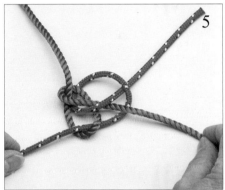

HARNESS BEND

Used widely for joining leather straps in the days of horse-drawn vehicles, this bend can be used to join cord-like strips of a wide range of materials.

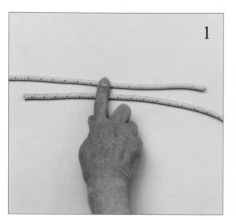

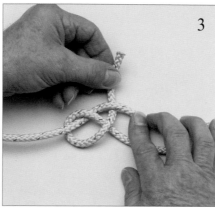

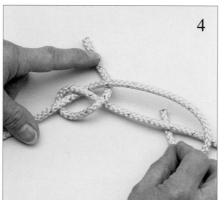

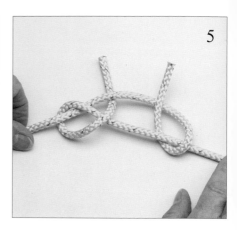

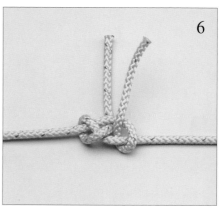

1 Place the two ends parallel but facing in opposite directions.

2 Take one end over the other cord and around under it.

3 Lead it over itself and under the other cord.

4,5 Pass the second cord over the first. Bring it around under the first and up over its standing part.

6 Support the form while tightening the knot.

DOUBLE HARNESS BEND

More aesthetically pleasing than the previous bend and possibly a little more secure.

TIP Contrive to cross the red w'end in front of the purple w'end for a more stable and secure knot (see pictures 4 and 5).

1,2 Start exactly as for the harness bend.

3 Carry out the same steps as in Stages 1 and 2, using the other working end. This makes the knot symmetrical.

4,5 Support and tighten carefully.

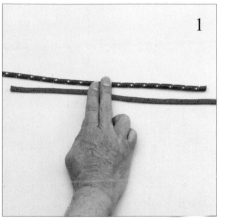

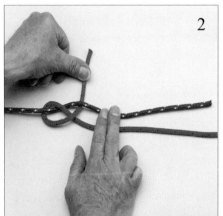

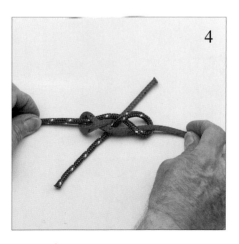

ADJUSTABLE BEND

Unlike most bends, the two sections remain apart in normal use, only to slide together when a sudden load is applied. This eases the strain and reduces the shock.

Canadian climber Robert Chisnall is credited with having devised this bend more than 20 years ago.

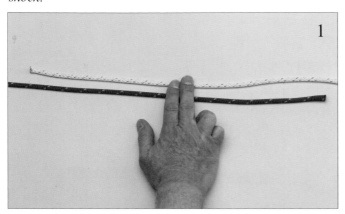

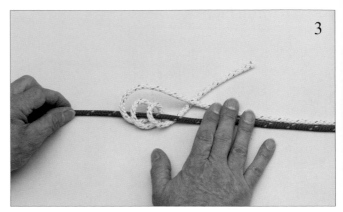

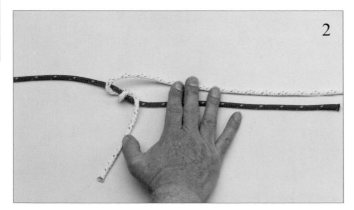

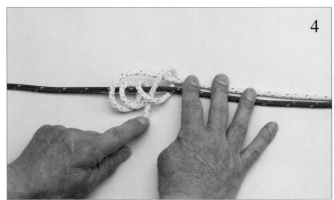

1 Lay the two cords parallel to one another but facing in opposite directions.

2 Twist one cord twice around the other wrapping towards the end.

3 Bring the w'end under both the wrapped cord and itself.

4 Lead the w'end over and down, trapping it under its own final turn.

WHAT KNOT?

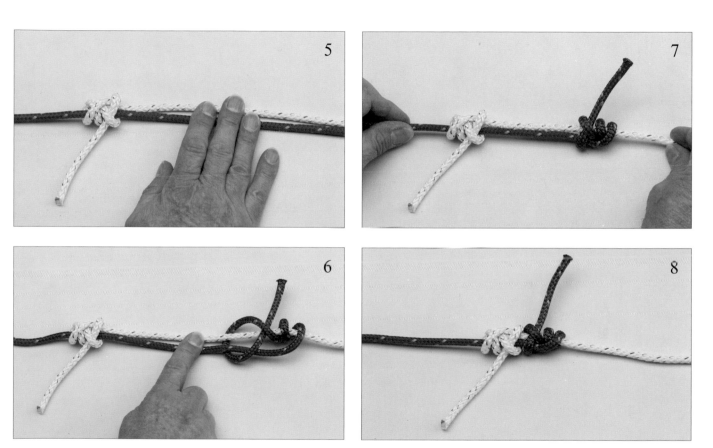

$5,6$ Move a short distance along the cords and repeat stages 2,3 and 4. This will produce a symmetrical knot.

$7,8$ Work each half of the knot tight.

MODIFIED TARBUCK KNOT

The accomplished Canadian climber Rob Chisnall devised this version and has used it for more than 30 years to secure Tyrolean traverse and highlines around trees and structural pillars. In slow-pull tests to failure, it was rated 100 per cent efficient.

OUTDOOR PURSUITS

CAVING & CLIMBING

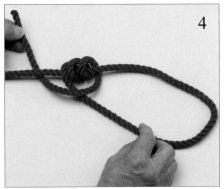

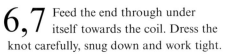

1 Make a loop of the size required.

2 Take the working end around the standing part and wrap it three times, working into the loop.

3 Come out and away from the loop.

4 Bring the w'end over the standing part.

5 Pass the w'end under the standing part.

6,7 Feed the end through under itself towards the coil. Dress the knot carefully, snug down and work tight.

ALPINE BUTTERFLY LOOP

This fixed loop has many applications, apart from its original use in mountaineering. It is especially useful in that it will take a load on any of its three limbs without distorting.

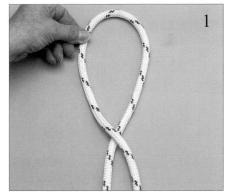

1 Hold the rope where you intend to position the centre of the loop. Let the ends hang down.

2 Twist your wrist so that the ends cross.

3 Twist again in the same direction.

4 Support the upper crossing and allow the top loop to fall forward and down.

5 Ensure the centre of the loop is now below the second crossing. Take the centre of the loop, pass it under the lower crossing and up through the gap between the crossings.

6 Still holding the top of the loop, allow the sides to fall into place and work tight.

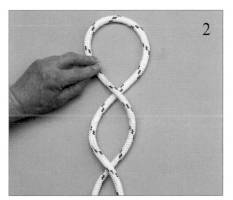

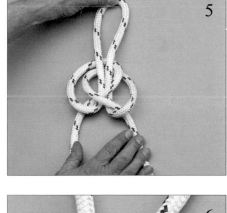

FARMER'S LOOP

Given its name in a pamphlet on American farms in 1912, this is a useful knot to know and one that is fun to tie.

3 Take the new middle turn and lift it over the turn near the tips of the fingers.

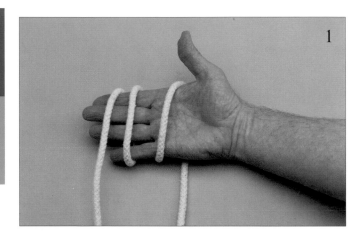

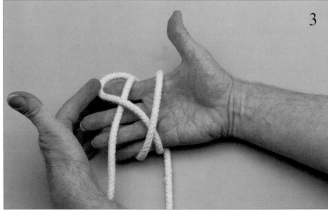

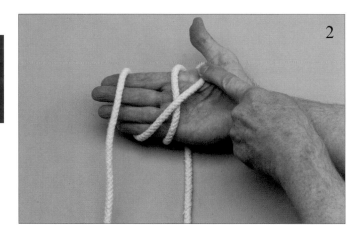

1 Take three loose turns around the palm so that the final turn near the tips of the fingers is towards you.

2 Lift the middle turn and place it over the turn nearest the thumb.

4 The new middle turn is now lifted towards the thumb as in stage 3.

WHAT KNOT?

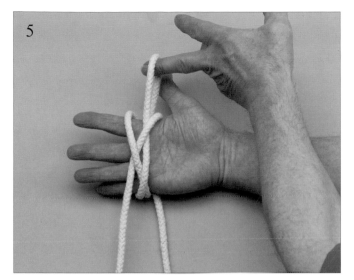

5,6 The latest middle turn is lifted to form the size of loop required, and the turns are carefully removed from the hand.

7 Snug the knot up and tighten.

MANHARNESS LOOP

This very old knot was used to form hauling loops in tow or drag lines for moving carts or cannon when horses were unavailable or required assistance. It is useful because it can be tied in the bight.

1 Make an overhand loop.

2 Bring the upper arm of the loop underneath the loop.

3 Push the right side of the loop under this cord and up out of the loop.

4,5 Holding the two ends, pull on the loop to tighten.

WHAT KNOT?

SISTER LOOPS

Useful when suspending items, these also have rescue applications.

3 Pass the w'end behind the initial bight.

4 Take the w'end back down through the eye.

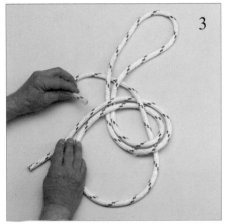

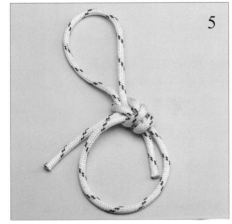

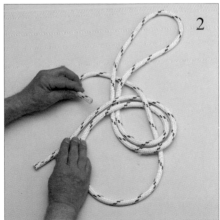

1 Double a length of cord and form an underhand loop, leaving a bight large enough for your requirements.

2 Lead the w'end under both strands of the loop, then up and out. Adjust the loops to the sizes required.

5,6 Adjust to the dimensions required. Dress, snug and tighten.

165

SPANISH BOWLINE

A useful old knot once used in rescue. However, the 'victim' must know how to utilize it to prevent further mishap, as one loop can slide into the other.

NOTE *BE CAUTIOUS WHEN USING THIS KNOT. If the double loops are near the end of the rope, secure the short leg to the longer leg using a double-overhand knot.*

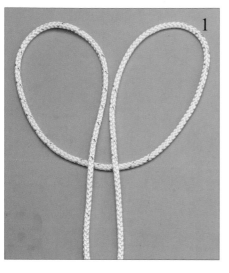

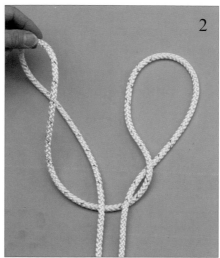

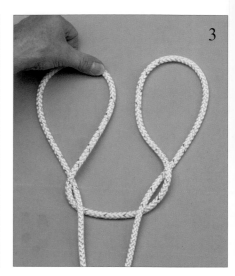

1 Take a large bight and drop it behind the legs to form two loops.

2 Give each loop an equal but opposite twist – anticlockwise for the left loop, clockwise for the right.

3 Take the left loop near its centre. Make sure the twists stay in place.

4 Crossing under the right standing part, pass the left loop through the right loop. This will twist the legs.

5 Straighten them, but retain all other twists.

WHAT KNOT?

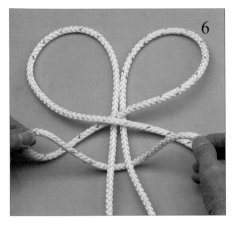

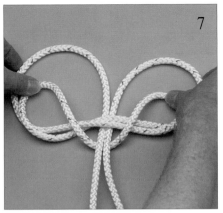

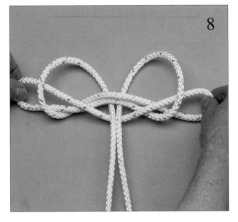

6 Pull on the sides of the lower crossed loop.

7 Twist the sides to form eyes by turning the left loop anticlockwise and the right one clockwise.

8 Place these eyes over the lower cords of the large loops.

9 Pull the eyes through the corresponding loops until they are of the required size.

10 Dress the knot and tighten. (Both sides of the knot are also shown below.)

JURY MAST KNOT

Originally used at the top of an improvised mast to enable stays to be attached, this attractive knot is now most often seen as decoration.

The improvised mast or flagpole is fitted into the six-sided hole in the centre of the knot before it is pulled tight, then stays or guy ropes are attached to the loops. The loose ends may be joined to form a fourth loop, or, if long enough, used for extra stays.

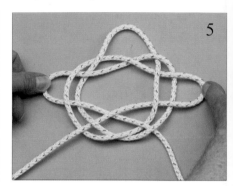

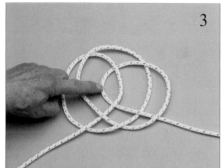

1 Form three overhand loops and enlarge the middle loop.

2 Overlap the edges of the loops, right over the middle and middle over the left.

3 Continue the overlap of the outer loops so that the inner edge of the left loop goes over the inner edge of right loop.

4 Weave the loop edges over then under (for the other loop under then over) until they emerge from the far sides of the loops.

5 Continue to pull the side loops thus formed until big enough.

6 Extend the centre loop upwards until it is the required size. Dress the knot.

BOATING & SAILING

CRAFTS

TIMBER HITCH/KILLICK HITCH

An old and simple hitch used to haul timber from the felling site, this is also used to secure the lower end of the string on a traditional English longbow.

The addition of a half hitch a short way along the load, in the direction of pull, converts the timber hitch into a Killick hitch, allowing for a greater degree of directional control.

Tied around any rough-shaped rock, it also makes an improvised anchor.

TIP It may sometimes be easier to put the half hitch on first, then the timber hitch.

BOATING & SAILING

HOUSE & GARDEN

OUTDOOR PURSUITS

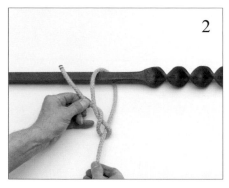

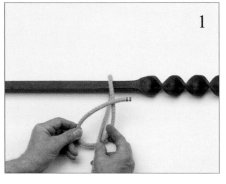

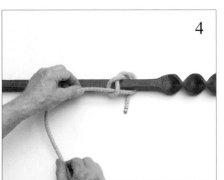

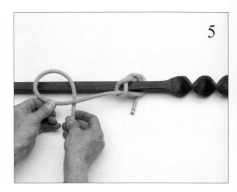

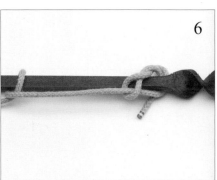

1 Pass the end of the cord around the object, bringing the w'end back over the standing part.

2 Lead the w'end into the loop.

3 Wrap the working part several times around its own side of the loop.

4 Pull taut. The wraps will lock against the load.

5 Move along the load in the direction of pull.

6 Form a half hitch around the load.

WHAT KNOT?

SLIP-and-GRIP HITCH (end-loaded, one-way)

Also known as the extended French Prusik knot, when tied in climber's 1-inch (2.5-cm) webbing, the knot is supposed to slip when the initial shock load is applied, but to grip once the shock has eased.

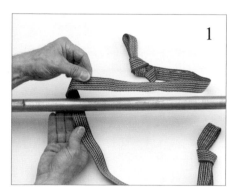

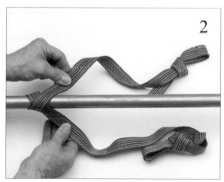

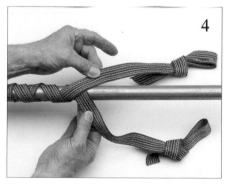

1 Middle the webbing and place it across the main rope.

2 Bring the ends around in opposite directions and cross one over the other.

3 Continue the wrappings with the crossings alternating.

4 The crossing that goes over at one wrap will go under the next.

5,6 Keep the diamond-shaped gaps between crossings as small as possible. Tie loops in the ends of the webbing and join with a karabiner.

171

SLIP-and-GRIP HITCH (centre-loaded, two-way)

Similar to the previous hitch, but tied with a continuous loop sling.

SAFETY NOTE Repeated use of either knot will make the sling shiny and slippery, reducing friction and grip. Discard sling as soon as this becomes apparent.

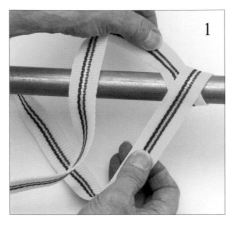

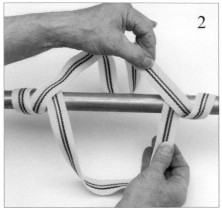

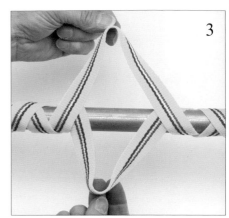

1 Place the sling under the beam. Bring the sides up and cross them.

2 Repeat the wrappings, alternating the crossings.

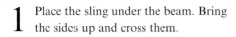

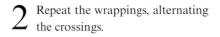

3 As one end is wrapped, the other end of the sling will mirror the wrapping. Make sure the wraps lie flat and alternate.

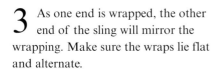

4,5 Continue until the sling is used up and there are only two small loops in the centre. Pass a karabiner through these loops.

WHAT KNOT?

MUNTER FRICTION KNOT

This friction hitch for kernmantel rope provides an effective means of controlling a belay. It can reverse its orientation, allowing control at all times in either direction.

1 Make a bight in the rope.

2 Twist the bight to form a loop.

3 Twist the loop again in the same direction.

4,5 Pass a locking karabiner around the standing part and into the loop.

6 Close up the hitch.

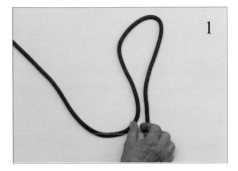

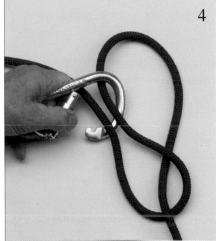

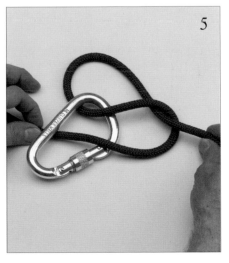

DOUBLE MUNTER FRICTION HITCH

An additional turn around the karabiner increases friction, thus providing more control.

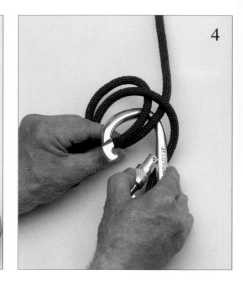

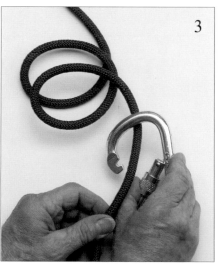

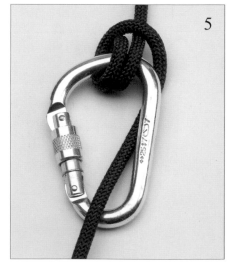

1 Make a loop.

2 Make a second loop on top of the first.

3 Open the locking karabiner and pass it over the rope.

4 With the standing part of the rope inside the karabiner and below the gate, twist the upper part of the karabiner. Bring it through the double loops from back to front.

5 Remove slack.

OUTDOOR PURSUITS

CAVING & CLIMBING

What Knot?

PRUSIK KNOT

Devised as a means of repairing the strings of musical instruments, this knot is now best known as a self-rescue knot for climbers. Given downward pressure, the knot jams, but when the load is removed the grip releases and the knot may be slid into a new position along the rope.

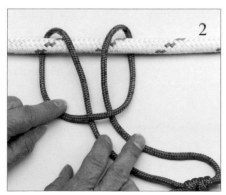

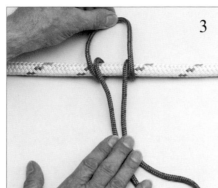

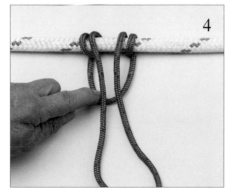

1 Take an endless loop of cord, thinner than the climbing rope. Pass a bight over the climbing rope.

2 Lead the standing part of the loop through the bight.

3 Raise the first bight.

4 Take the raised bight over the rope and down behind.

5 Feed the large loop through the bight again.

6 Dress the knot. Tighten.

MAVERICKS & MUTATIONS

DOUBLE PRUSIK KNOT

A Prusik knot with an extra wrap to give greater grip. It is possible to use even more wraps, but nowadays other slip-and-grip knots have become more popular.

NOTE It is quite easy to tie this knot one-handed, but as your life will depend on it, a lot of practice is required.

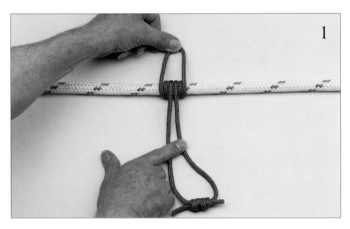

1 Tie an ordinary Prusik knot, but do not tighten. Raise the bight.

2 Pass the bight behind the climbing rope and bring the standing loop through the bight.

3 Dress the knot, ensuring the wraps lie flat without crossings. Tighten.

OUTDOOR PURSUITS

CAVING & CLIMBING

ASHER'S BOTTLE SLING

*Devised by the late Harry Asher, this knot provides a simple method of hanging
or slinging bottles to make them easy to carry.*

1 Start as for a Prusik knot. With a loop of cord, take a bight around the neck of the bottle.

2 Lead the loop through, raise the bight, and repeat.

3 Pull down the bight.

4 Twist the bight to form a loop. Pass the standing loop up through the newly-formed loop.

5 Tighten.

177

TRUCKER'S HITCH

Also known as the waggoner's hitch or lorry driver's dolly knot, this ancient hitch is just what is needed to secure a canoe on a roof rack or to tension a line. It is tied in the bight, but the far end of the rope must be secured before passing it over the load for tightening.

NOTE The cord is usually passed to the next anchor point along the side of the truck, thrown over the load and the process repeated on the other side until the load is secure.

Many will advocate a second overhand loop at Stage 2, crossing over and locking the first. There are several variations found around the world.

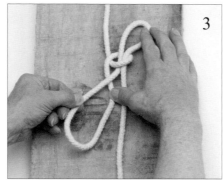

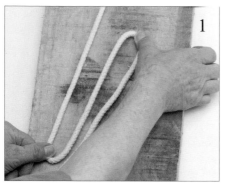

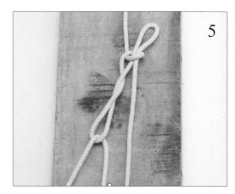

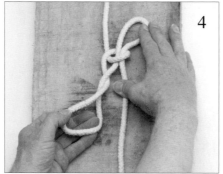

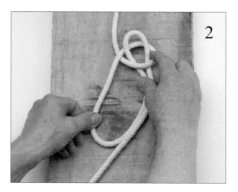

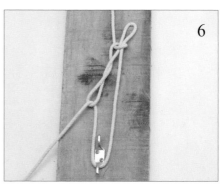

1 Make a suitably-sized bight in the rope and bring it up alongside the standing part.

2 Form an anti-clockwise loop in the standing part and pass it over the bight.

3 While supporting the upper part, put a twist into the lower loop.

4 Give a second twist.

5,6 Reach through the lowest loop, and take hold of the standing part. Pull it through to make a bight, which is hooked over the anchor point. Haul taut on the working part and secure with a half hitch at the anchor.

WHAT KNOT?

POLDO TACKLE

This self-working tackle can be used in many situations on both land and sea to apply tension. Because it is so easy to slacken off, it is valuable as a quick-release lashing. This cordage contrivance is named after sailing instructor, Poldo Izzo.

1

3

2

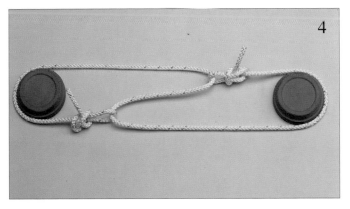

4

1 Make a loop on one end of the cord. Any loop will do. Pass the other end through the loop to form a noose. Tie the second end back into the noose with another loop knot to make a matching noose.

2 Arrange the first noose over one anchor and the second noose over the item to be tensioned.

3 To tension – pull the loop knots away from one another.

4 To release – push the loop knots towards one another.

179

VERSA TACKLE

This DIY device was invented by George Aldridge and first described by him in Knotting Matters, Number 13, October 1985.

HOUSE & GARDEN

OUTDOOR PURSUITS

CAVING & CLIMBING

1 Tie a loop in one end of the cord. With this loop near one anchor point, lead the cord around the anchor, over to the second point, and tie another loop close to the fixed point.

2 Lead the long end of the rope through the first loop and back towards the second loop.

3,4 Pass the cord through the second loop. Repeat steps 2 and 3 until there are three complete coils held between the loops.

5 Pull on the free end and the tackle should tighten up considerably. It should be self-locking but secure, with a half hitch for safety. To release, unthread the working end for a short distance. Ease the slack around until the tackle loosens.

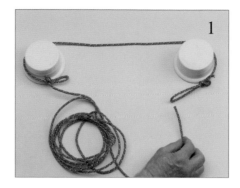

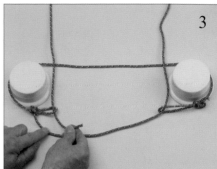

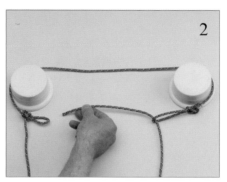

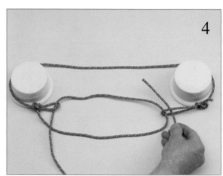

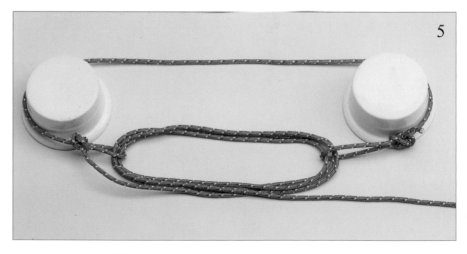

BALE SLING HITCH

This simple hitch is tied using a continuous loop. A cargo strop or looped climbing sling may be used to suspend a compact, firm load from a girder or beam.

3 Feed the rest of the sling through the bight.

4,5 Dress the sling and tighten.

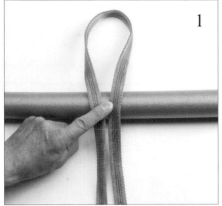

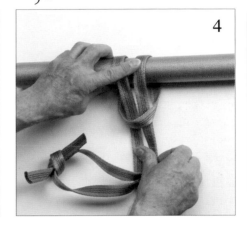

1 Place the sling across the beam.

2 Pass a bight down behind the beam.

HOUSE & GARDEN

OUTDOOR PURSUITS

CRAFTS

RING HITCH, DOUBLE-ENDED

This hitch is interesting because it can be untied using either end of the looped cord.

1 Select your rings and form a continuous loop with the cord.

2 Pass a bight of the loop through the first ring and bring it back.

3 Feed the long part of the loop through the bight.

4 Pass the loop through the second ring and bring back to the first ring.

5 Take the end of the loop under the part that crosses the cords.

6 Lift it over the first ring, spread the sides, and let the loop come down behind the ring.

7 Gently pull tight.

NOTE The apparent reef knot may be positioned anywhere it is required by careful manipulation of the cords. To undo, raise either of the crossing cords over the top of the first ring and the hitch will fall apart.

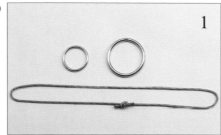

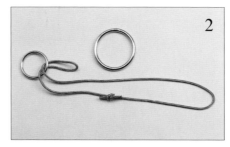

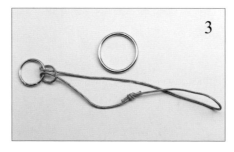

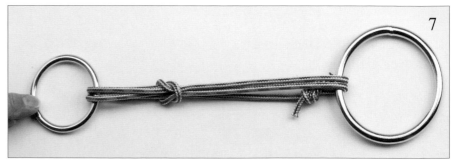

BULL HITCH (tied with an end)

Called the bull hitch, because it is a stronger and beefier version of a cow hitch (page 191), this is useful for suspending objects in the garage or workplace.

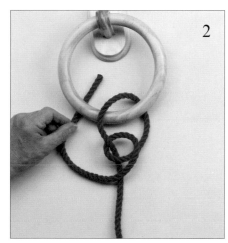

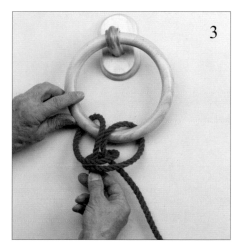

1 Pass the cord through the ring from front to back.

2 Bring it down and form a half hitch around the standing part.

3 Lead the w'end in front of the standing part and through the ring, but this time from back to front.

4 Feed the w'end down through the eye of the half hitch alongside the standing part. Tighten.

BULL HITCH TWO (tied in the bight)

When the anchor or hanging point takes the open form of a nail or hook, instead of being closed like a ring, this knot may be tied in the bight.

1 Form a bight and let it drop forward to give two loops with the left slightly larger than the right.

2 Supporting the loops at the crossing, twist the larger loop completely over and around the smaller loop so that the outside leg of the larger loop passes completely behind the smaller loop and back in front of the standing part.

3 Straighten the loops.

4 Pass the anchor part through the loops.

5 Tighten.

WHAT KNOT?

CATSPAW

A secure hitch to fasten a strop or sling to a hook, so that a load may be hoisted safely. The knot is known to have been used by the ancient Greeks and may be tied in almost any size of cord or rope, from fishing lines to cables.

4 Even up the loops.

5 Pass the two eyes at the top of the loops over the hook. Tighten by loading the standing parts.

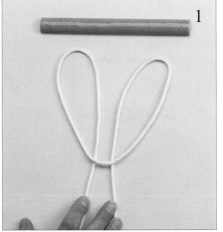

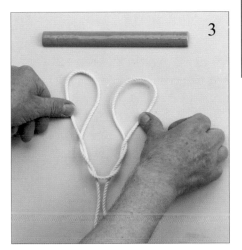

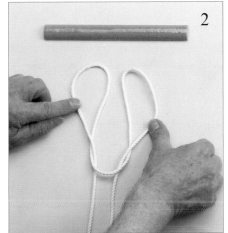

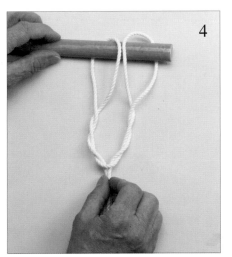

1 Form a bight in the sling or cord and let it drop forward to make two loops.

2 Twist the left-hand loop clockwise and the right-hand loop anti-clockwise.

3 Continue to twist the loops evenly, so that each loop has exactly the same number of twists, but in opposite directions.

COLLARED HITCH

This modification of the Ossel hitch (page 198) gives a robust knot that grips strongly and withstands a pull form any direction.

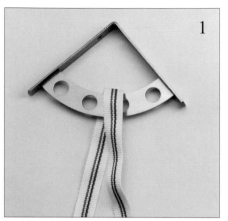

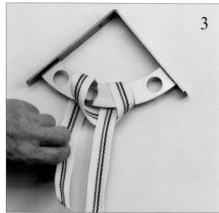

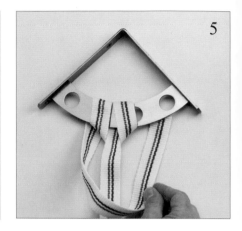

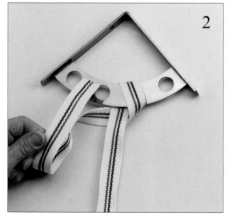

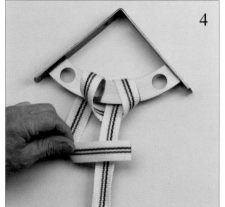

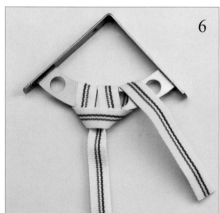

1 Bring the w'end up behind the anchor and over to the front.

2 Lead the w'end behind the standing part, up in front of the anchor.

3 Go over it and down again.

4 Come in front of the standing part.

5 Now go up behind the anchor.

6 Come over the top of the anchor. This completes the collar.

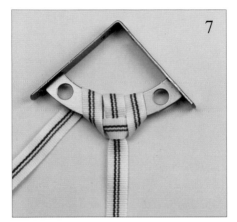

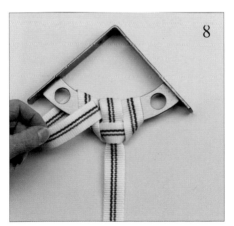

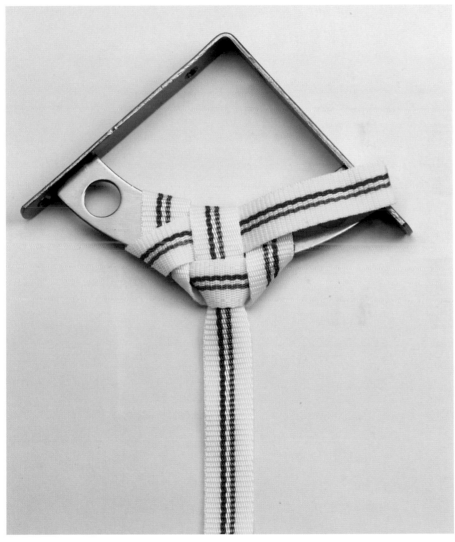

7   Looking from behind, lead the
w'end around.

8   Tuck the w'end under the central
turn to secure it. Dress and tighten.

GAFF TOPSAIL HALYARD BEND

This nautically-named knot is in fact a hitch, but sailors 'bend' ropes to rings or spars. It is secure when pulled at right angles to the point of attachment.

1,2 Pass the cord twice around the anchor. This makes a full round turn.

3 Take the w'end behind the standing part.

4 Bring the w'end up and tuck it behind both parts of the round turn. Tighten.

WHAT KNOT?

HALYARD HITCH

Known nautically as a topsail (sometimes studding sail) halyard bend, some finish it off by coming over two turns and under one. Both variations will hold.

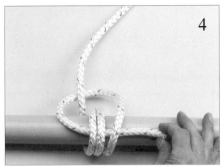

1 Bring the cord under the anchor and pass it over the anchor.

2 Pass the w'end over the anchor again.

3 Bring the w'end around again and up behind the standing part.

4 Come around the standing part and feed the w'end under all three turns.

5,6 Reversing direction, take the w'end over one turn and under the next two turns. Tighten.

CAMEL HITCH

Many knots are not as secure when wet as they are dry. Camels are ruminants and tend to slobber, consequently the knot used to secure a valuable camel to a picket line must be capable of resisting nibbling and chewing when sodden.

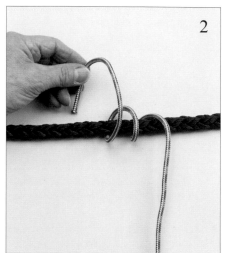

1 Take a turn from front to back around the picket line.

2 Complete two more turns.

3 Bring the w'end in front of the standing part and behind the picket line.

4,5 Form a half hitch followed by a second half hitch. Close the turns up, dress and tighten.

COW HITCH

A simple general-purpose hitch that is not very secure and should not be trusted with anything valuable.

To make this into a safe, useful knot, a small modification is shown which upgrades it to a pedigree cow hitch.

1 Pass the line over the anchor – here it goes through the middle hole of the brick. Bring the end down at the back, around in front of the standing part, and back behind the anchor. It is now brought up over the anchor, back through the hole, and is fed through the loop alongside the standing part. Pull tight.

2,3 To modify, do not pull tight just yet. Take the w'end and pass it between the anchor and the two turns. If easy untying is desired, pass a bight instead of the w'end, thus forming a draw-loop. Tighten.

NOTE. The form of the basic cow hitch will be well known, being similar to other knots, such as the ring hitch. It is also known as a lark's head and will be familiar to macramé and tatting enthusiasts.

If the end of one of the cords in a reef knot is pulled sharply, the knot will spill into a lark's head and a straight line, and the lark's head can then slide off the other cord. This explains why the reef knot should never be used to join cord in a situation where a life might be at risk.

HIGHWAYMAN'S HITCH

While it is fun to associate this knot with anti-heroes such as Dick Turpin or Jesse James, it would be foolish to believe either was the originator of this hitch.

It does, however, make an effective quick-release animal tether or boat mooring, that unties with just a pull on the loose end.

3,4 Pass this third bight under the second bight, locking it into place. Dress and tighten. Give a sharp tug on the protruding, unloaded cord to untie.

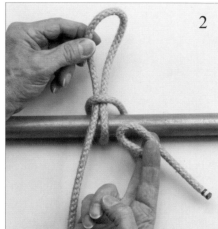

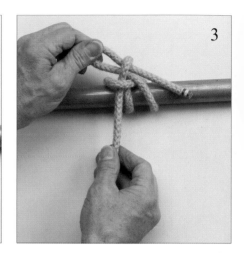

1 Form a bight and pass it behind the anchor. Make a second small bight in the cord leading to the load.

2 Bring the second (load side) bight up in front of the anchor and pass it through the first bight. Close the first bight by pulling on the non-load side and then form another bight in the non-loadbearing side.

WHAT KNOT?

HOISTING HITCH

Although the pictures show a hammer being prepared for hauling aloft, this hitch is used for hoisting sections of oil-well drilling bits. It provides a reliable hitch for hauling or hoisting long, heavy loads.

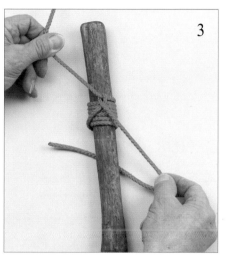

1 Wrap about eight turns around the object to be lifted, working away from the direction of lift.

2 Bring the w'end up diagonally across all the turns.

3 Take the w'end behind the standing part. Bring it back down to the bottom of the wrapping.

4 Take a final turn and lock off with a half hitch. Tighten every turn carefully before loading.

LIGHTERMAN'S HITCH

Used by Thames lightermen when towing dumb (engine-less) barges, this rapidly constructed but strong hitch may now be found in many places where a heavy-duty but rapidly removable hitch is required. Access to the top of the bollard or stake is essential, as is a long enough working end.

BOATING & SAILING

HOUSE & GARDEN

OUTDOOR PURSUITS

1 Take a turn or two around the bollard to provide enough friction to control the load.

2 Form a bight in the working part.

3 Pass the bight under the standing (loaded) part.

4 Lift the bight and drop it over the bollard. Pull on the working part to close the bight.

5,6 Coming from the other side of the standing part, bring another bight in the working part up and over the bollard. Pull tight.

7 Bring the working end over the top of the standing part, forming a loop around it.

8 Take a final turn around the bollard and let the end hang loose.

BOATING & SAILING

HOUSE & GARDEN

OUTDOOR PURSUITS

KNUTE KNOT

Not, as one might think, named after a Scandinavian king, but in honour of the favourite marlinspike of American master rigger, Brion Toss. When working aloft, all tools should be fitted with a lanyard to prevent damage below, and the possible loss of the tool if it should fall. It also saves a tiring and time consuming descent to the deck to retrieve the item.

3 The end of the lanyard is brought around the tool and through the bight

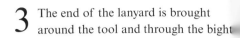

4,5 Pull gently to withdraw the bight, which will then be locked in place. A figure of eight as a stopper knot in the end of the cord will prevent the end from escaping.

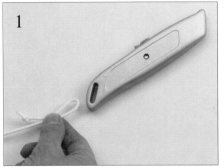

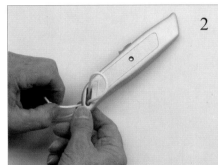

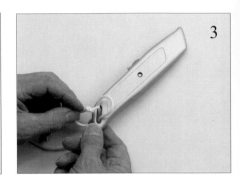

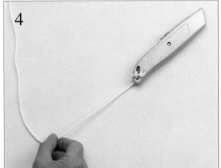

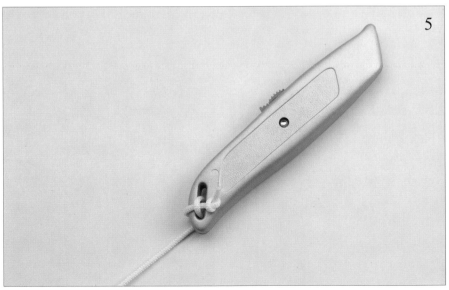

1 Form a bight in your lanyard, using cord that, doubled, will just go through the lanyard hole of the tool.

2 Pass the bight through the lanyard hole.

MOORING HITCH

A simple quick-release hitch that may be used for temporary moorings.

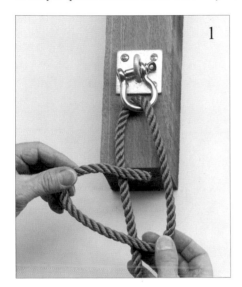

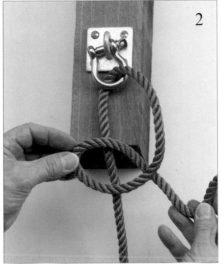

1 Pass the end of the line through the ring, returning it back towards you. Make a clockwise underhand loop.

2 Pass the loop over the standing part.

3,4 Form a bight in the working part. Weave the bight across the loop, going under the standing part and coming out on top of the loop. This is the locking draw-loop. Dress and tighten.

5 To undo, pull the free end of the locking draw-loop.

OSSEL HITCH

*From norsel, a Scottish fisherman's word for a gill net, this hitch once secured
the supporting ropes that connected the drift nets to the submerged footrope.
Shown here tied in webbing tape, it makes a quick, simple and secure fastening.*

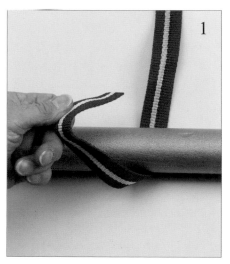

1 Come down behind the fixing point
and around to the front.

2 Pass the end up and behind the
standing part.

3 Come back to the front and down
again.

4 Bring the end up behind the fixing
point.

5 Pass over the first knot part and tuck
the end under the second knot part.
Tighten.

WHAT KNOT?

OSSEL KNOT

This knot secured the support ropes of the drift nets to the headrope. It is somewhat more secure than the Ossel hitch, as it was likely to be subjected to more severe battering by the waves.

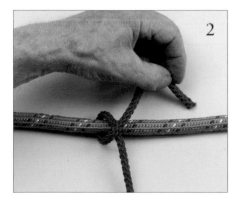

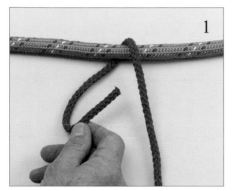

1 Take the working end up and over the headrope.

2 Bring the end around diagonally across in front of the standing part. Send it back down behind the headrope.

3 Lead the end up again alongside the first warp but between it and the standing part.

4 Continuing in the same direction, complete a further turn, but this time on the other side of the standing part.

5 Pull out a bight in the standing part, where it first crosses the headrope. Pass the working end through the bight.

6 Pull down on the standing part to trap the working end in place. Tighten.

199

CLIMBER'S COIL

There are many ways to complete the coiling of a rope. This method gives a coil that can be slung on the back, making it easy to carry. The resulting coil may not be the most attractive to look at, but it is quick and practical.

1 Find the two ends of the rope and keep them together. Move about three arm-spans along the rope and from there on make the coil as you find most convenient with a doubled rope.

2 When the coil is formed, start to wrap the two loose ends together tightly around the coil, commencing about one third of the way along.

3 Continue the wrapping, working towards the closest end of the coil.

4 After six tight wrapping turns have been taken, form a bight in the loose ends.

5 Pass the bight through the eye formed at the top of the coil.

6 Feed the two loose ends through the bight. Haul taut to lock the bight in place. The loose ends can then be used as shoulder straps to sling the coil onto the back, taking them back through the coil or around the waist as desired.

PILE or POST HITCH

Whenever a temporary barrier is erected, using a line supported by a row of posts, a knot is required at each post to stop the line from falling to the ground.

NOTE This hitch may be tied in cord, plastic tape or, as here, webbing.

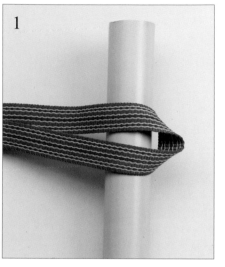

1 Make a bight in the tape.

2 Pass the bight in front of, and then behind the post.

3 Bring the bight forward beneath both standing parts. Loop it over the top of the post.

4,5 Adjust to give a taut line. Lead the line along to the next post and repeat the process until the barrier has been completed.

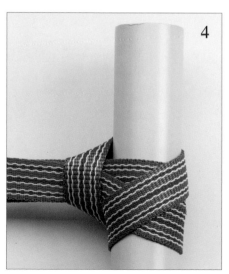

WHAT KNOT?

DOUBLE PILE or POST HITCH

This modification of the pile hitch allows a load to be applied from either standing part and also resists a pull towards the bight.

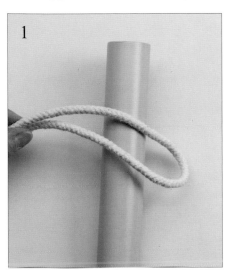

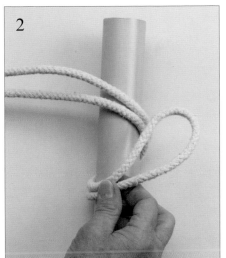

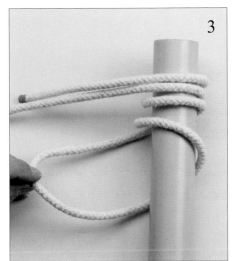

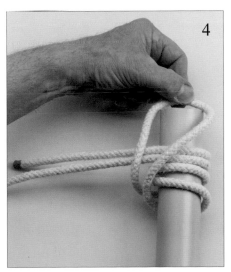

1 Form a bight in the cord.

2 Pass the bight around the post and out under the two standing parts.

3 Take the bight around the post a second time.

4,5 Bring the bight up and loop it over the top of the post. Dress carefully and tighten before applying a load.

SNUG HITCH

This hitch provides a secure hold that withstands a variable load, using even synthetic cords.

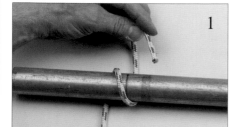

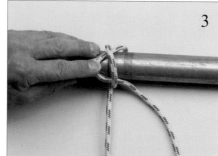

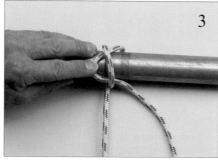

5,6 Come up in front outside the previous turn. Go over the first knot part and tuck under the next.

7 Tighten.

1 Pass the cord over the pole, around the back, and bring it to the front of the standing part.

2 Go down behind the pole on the other side of the standing part and up to cross in front of the standing part.

3,4 Tuck the working end under the first turn and go over the pole again.

FIREMAN'S COIL

Another way of completing a coil that allows it to be easily hung from the securing bight.

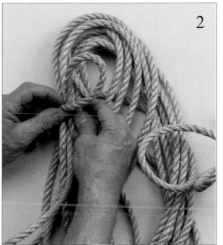

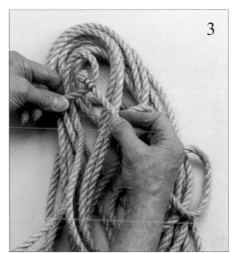

1 Coil the rope as convenient and bring both ends together. You only need one end, but it keeps the loose end tidy.

2 With one of the ends, make a small overhand loop, but allow a suitable length for working.

3 Lead the working end all around the coil, back through the loop, and through the eye at the top of the coil.

4,5 Arrange the resulting seizing neatly and snugly.

BRAID KNOT

With one strand, this attractive knot copies the common three-strand plait. It may be used for decoration, to shorten a rope, or as a makeshift handle on a suitcase.

1 Prepare a long underhand loop and arrange it to give three parallel lines.

2 Bring the free strand over the middle strand and lay it in the centre space.

3 Take the strand from the other side and cross it over to the middle.

4 Continue to take alternate outside strands and bring them to the centre.

5 As braiding continues, a mirror image is formed below the working area. Pull out the long working ends and untwist the tangle.

WHAT KNOT?

6 Continue braiding and untangling, pulling each step tight.

7 Tighten the braid until one loop remains at the end.

8 Feed the working end through this loop to lock and secure the braid.

SENNIT KNOT

In 1928, Wright and Magowan described this knot in the Alpine Journal. It was used to join hawser-laid climbing ropes of natural fibre, but seems to have disappeared for a time. It has now resurfaced as an effective knot to be used in modern climbing ropes and even in elastic shock cordage.

BOATING & SAILING

HOUSE & GARDEN

OUTDOOR PURSUITS

CAVING & CLIMBING

CRAFTS

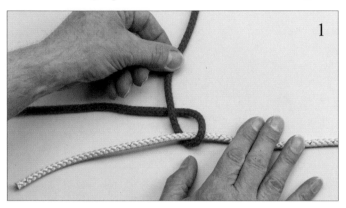

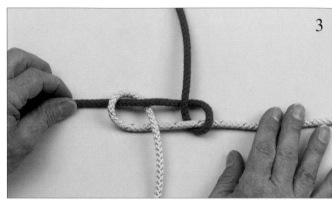

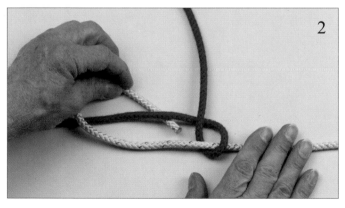

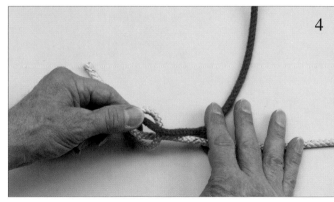

1 Make an overhand eye in one cord. Pass the other cord through the eye.

2 Take the end of the second cord over and behind the first cord.

3 This will produce another eye. The ends of the eyes should project on opposite sides.

4 Twist the left loop at 180° away from yourself.

5 Take the left working end behind the right working end and pass it through the right loop.

6,7 The right working end is now fed through the left loop. Tighten carefully.

TWIN SPLAYED LOOPS

This is another knot that produces two loops from which to sling or suspend an item.

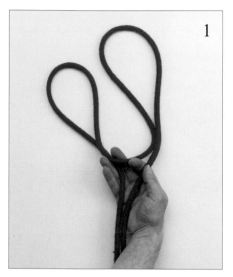

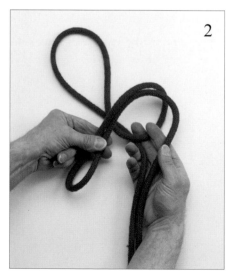

1 Bring the point of a long bight down to produce two ears.

2 Cross one ear across the stem of the other ear.

3 Cross the second ear over the first and over the two legs of the original bight, but leave a central gap.

4 Pass the legs of the original bight through the gap.

5 Pull through.

HOUSE & GARDEN

OUTDOOR PURSUITS

6 Arrange the knot to remove twists and untidy crossings. Work until snug and tighten.

TIP If, at Stage 1, you fold the legs of the bight over one ear, then continue the steps using the ears, you will not have as much rope to pull through the small gap at Stage 4.

6

CHINESE GOOD LUCK KNOT

This knot was named by Lydia Chen in 1981, though it had already possessed connotations of friendship among the Chinese people for some time. The technique for tying it is not unlike the method used for the Twin Splayed Loops.

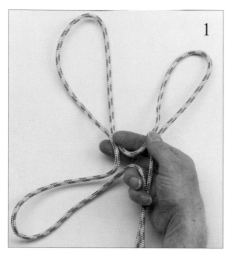

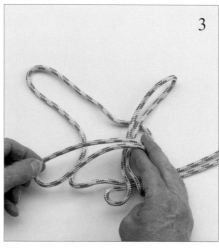

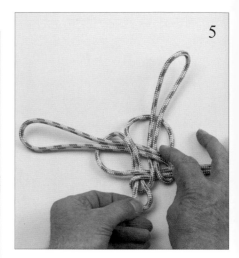

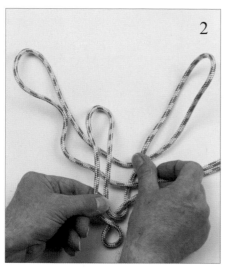

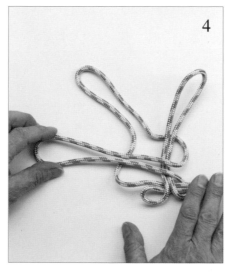

1 Double the cord. Fashion three long loops with two long ends.

2 Fold one loop across the stem of the next loop.

3 Cross the second loop over the first loop and over the stem of the third loop.

4 Cross the third loop over the second loop and over the two legs.

5 Cross the two legs over the third loop and through the eye (gap) made when the first loop began its travels. Pull the end through and tighten gently.

WHAT KNOT?

6,7,8,9 Repeat steps 1 to 5, but travelling in the opposite direction.

10 This is the tricky step. Gently dress the knot to remove unwanted twists and crossings. Even up the knot, ensuring the tension is equal in each arm. Gently tease out the small inner loops. Tighten.

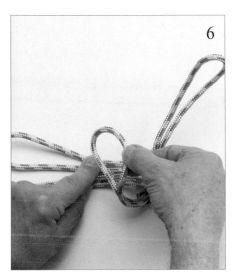

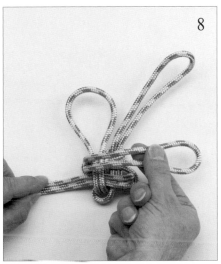

TURK'S HEAD (3 lead, 4 bight)

Turk's head is the name of a vast family of knots that are supposed to resemble a turban. Many have practical applications, but others are purely ornamental. They are distinguished by their number of 'leads' or plaited parts, and by the number of 'bights' or bumps on the rim. Frequently, the cord is followed around the knot two or three times to give a double- or triple-Turk's head.

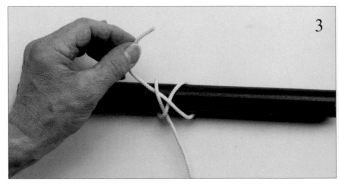

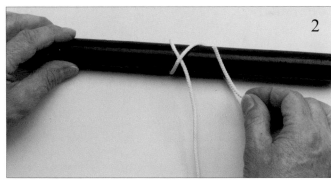

1 Take a turn around the pole from the front. Come back up in front, crossing over the standing part.

2 Take a second complete turn alongside the first.

3 Cross the w'end over the first cord it meets and then under the next. Lift the turn farthest from the w'end and carry it over the near turn.

4 Change the direction of the w'end and bring it over, then under successive turns.

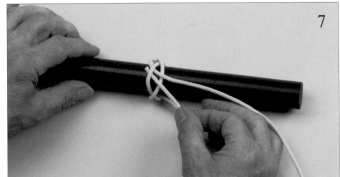

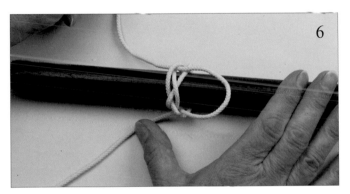

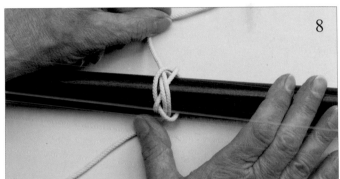

5 Change direction of the w'end again. Come over the next turn. You now meet the standing part going in the other direction.

6 Take the w'end alongside the standing part.

7,8,9 Follow around alongside the standing part until you have doubled or tripled the Turk's head. Work tight, concealing the ends within the knot.

TURK'S HEAD (3 lead, 5 bight)

Another member of the Turk's head family, but this time worked flat instead of around a pole. This way it produces an attractive drinks coaster, though it was originally used as a mat around a ringbolt to prevent damage to wooden decks. If a pole is introduced into the central hole, the mat may be collapsed and tightened to produce a ring knot.

1 Make a flat loop. With one end, form a bight and lay it over the loop. Feed the w'end under the standing part of the first loop.

2 Lead the w'end around and under the next cord.

3 Weave over, under, over, in the direction shown in the picture.

4 When the w'end is brought back to the start, the knot is complete. Now follow around to make a double- or triple-Turk's head. Dress and pull to make snug, making sure the turns lie flat.

TURK'S HEAD (5 lead, 4 bight)

Another member of the Turk's head family. As the size increases, so too does the difficulty, therefore patience is required to produce a satisfying result.

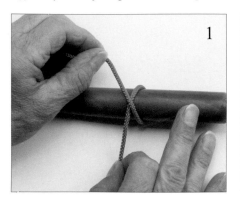

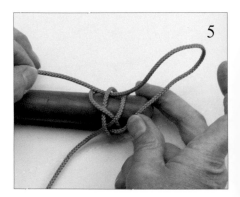

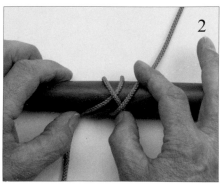

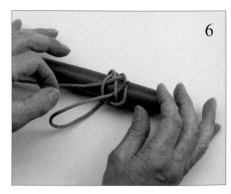

1 Take a turn from front to back.

2 Cross over the cord and take a further turn. Bring the w'end up to parallel the first turn on the outside.

3 Holding the first turn in place, feed the w'end under the first turn, over the second, and then go down behind. Bring the end up on the outside of the standing part.

4 Lead it under the first cord it meets and over the second cord. You now have two parallel cords, side by side, going under together.

5 Holding everything firmly in place, lead the w'end over the next cord, under the central cord, and over the outside cord. Note that you have come over two cords at the start of this stage. Do not let them move out of place.

218

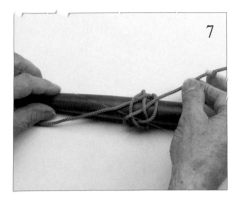

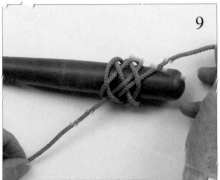

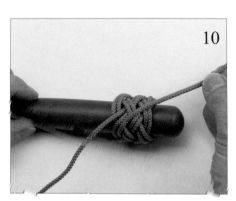

6 Continue to make a further turn but bring the end up inside the standing part. Go parallel to the first cord, between the two parallel cords of Stage 4, and weave over, under, over.

7 Change direction again and weave under, over, under.

8 This next weave should bring you back to the standing part.

9,10 Work around to double or triple the knot. Work out the slack. Tighten.

TIP Add another coloured cord to create an eye-catching effect.

SPANISH RING KNOT

Having mastered the Turk's head, the Spanish ring knot, often tied in leather or rawhide thonging, is a logical next step. This knot starts with a 5-bight, 3-lead Turk's head and modifies it to produce a ring that will never shake loose, with 8 bights, 5 leads, and an over-2/under-2 weave.

1 Make a turn from front to back and bring it up to cross over the standing part.

2 Continue to form a second turn that comes up inside the standing part.

3 Lead the w'end under, then over the turns.

4 Pull the turn coming from the standing part under the turn next to it.

5 Take the w'end under and over again.

6 Pull the turn you previously moved under its neighbour again.

7 Bring the w'end under this turn and up over the next turn.

8 When the w'end goes under the next turn it will meet the standing part and the 5B x 3L Turk's head is complete.

9 Pull the w'end out of its last tuck.

10 Pass it over and along the other side of the standing part and under the same part of the knot as the standing part.

11 Rotate the knot in your hand as needed to get a clear view. Pass the outside strand under the next bight.

12 Go over two strands and under the next bight.

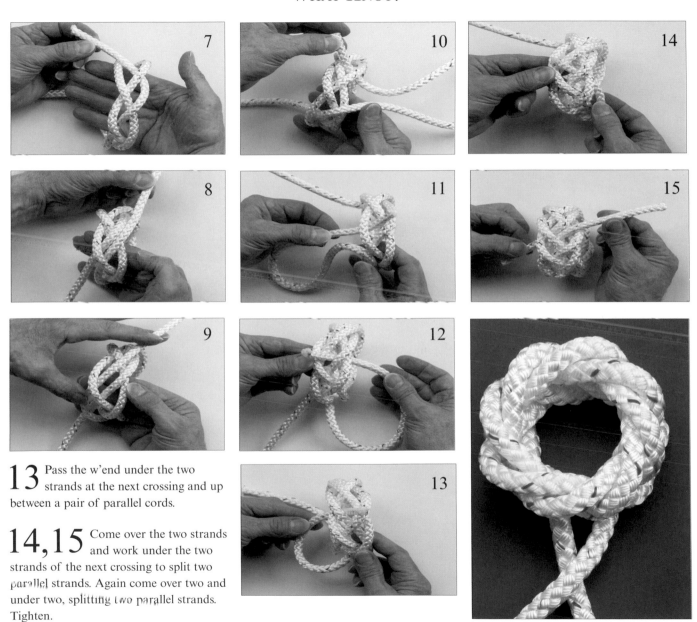

13 Pass the w'end under the two strands at the next crossing and up between a pair of parallel cords.

14,15 Come over the two strands and work under the two strands of the next crossing to split two parallel strands. Again come over two and under two, splitting two parallel strands. Tighten.

OCEAN PLAIT MAT

Mats are always useful to protect decks from damage and to provide a firm foothold in a companionway, while in a doorway, they are something on which to wipe your boots. This attractive mat is one of the easiest to make.

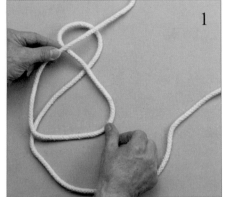

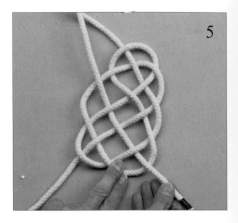

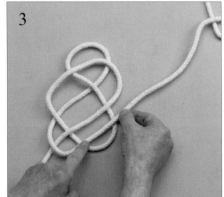

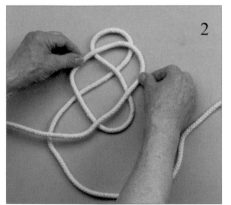

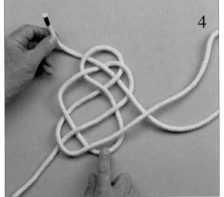

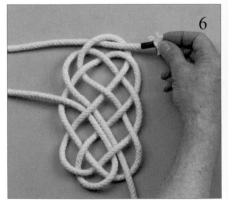

1 Bring the end up and lay it over the top loop, then down over the lower loop.

2 Using the other end, formerly the standing end but which will now be the working end, lead it up over the new standing part and under both parts of the nearest loop.

3 Pass the w'end diagonally upwards, weaving over, under, over, under.

4 Bring the w'end around and weave back in the gap between the diagonals, going over, under, over, under.

5 Turn the standing end around under the mat, roughly to mirror the other end, and follow through alongside the original lead to double the mat.

Sidebar tabs: BOATING & SAILING · HOUSE & GARDEN · CRAFTS

6 Use the other end, if long enough, to follow around to triple the mat. Work the slack through, keeping the mat flat.

7,8 The ends may be secured where they meet, preferably in the centre, by sewing through the cord. For added stability, the entire mat may be sewn, turn by turn, using strong twine.

KNIFE LANYARD KNOT

Also known as the two-stranded diamond knot, this looks attractive and makes a secure closure for a loop from which to suspend a knife or tool.

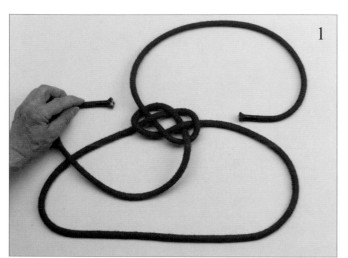

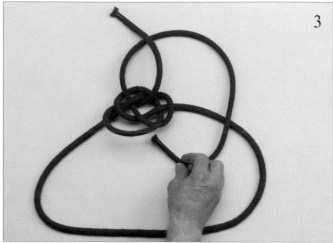

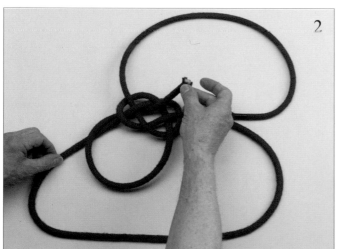

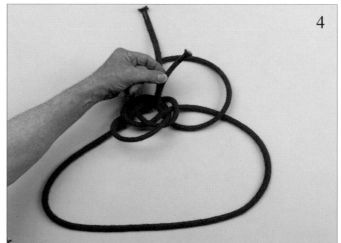

WHAT KNOT?

1 Middle your lanyard cord. The doubled cord should be long enough to allow you to work with a tool at arms length without being too tight or too slack. Tie a Carrick Bend (see pages 154–155) near the middle, enclosing a loop of suitable size, with the ends coming out on opposite sides.

2 Support the Carrick Bend so that the loop hangs down and the ends go out at the sides.

3 Take one end, bring it all the way around to the outside of the other side of the Carrick Bend.

4 Go under the bend and come up through the central diamond-shaped hole. Do the same with the other end. The ends are brought around in the natural direction in which they are pointing. In these pictures it is clockwise.

5,6 Hold both sides of the loop and both working ends close to the knot and gently pull. Work any slack through and tidy up any uneven crossings. Pull taut when all is correctly arranged.

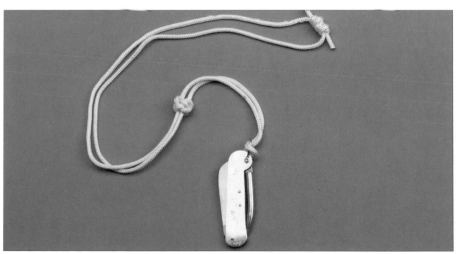

CHINESE CROSS KNOT

This is only one of many names by which this knot in known. It is also known in Great Britain as the square knot, and by a variety of names in America, where a square knot is a reef knot. This is an attractive way to secure a knotted scarf.

5 Gently close up and manipulate the parts to lie evenly.

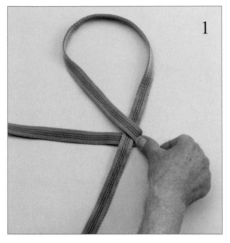

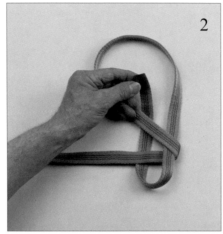

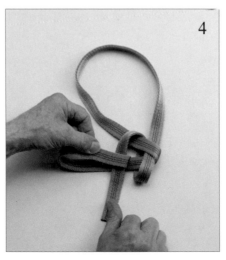

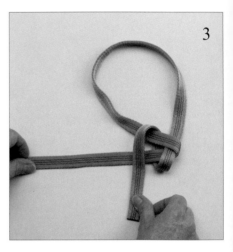

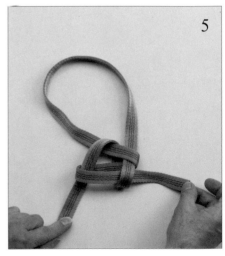

1 Form a loop and fold the standing part at right angles under the working part.

2 Lead the working end under both standing parts, leaving a small bight at the turn.

3 Bring the w'end up through the loop and back down parallel to the upward part

4 Take the standing part, fold it over, and bring it back through the small bight left behind at Stage 2.

BELOW: Detail of front.
BOTTOM: Detail of back.

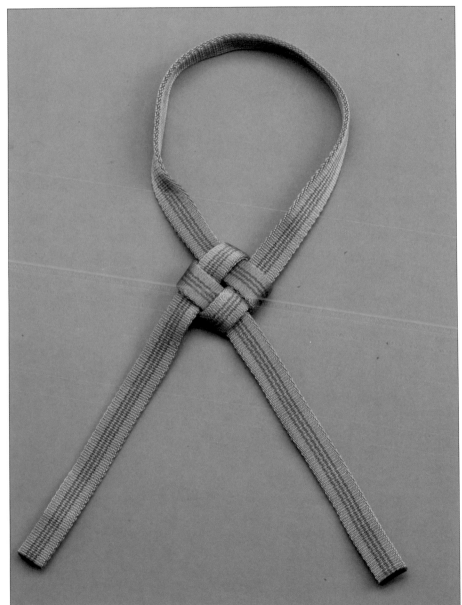

227

CHINESE CLOVERLEAF

*An ornamental knot that looks good and is associated, like many others, with
good luck.*

 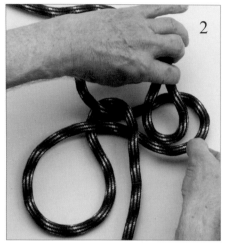 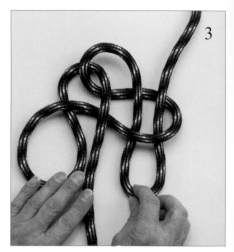

1 Form a bight in the cord. In one of the legs form another bight. Bring the second bight up and pass underneath the first bight. Allow enough slack to create an eye at the turn.

2 Bring the working part over the top of the knot and make another bight.

3 Pass this bight through the loop of the second bight.

4 Lead the working end around. Feed it through the first loop, over under, over, over into the next loop.

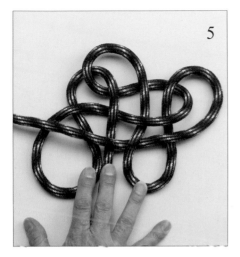

5 Go into this loop, then feed under the outer cord.

6 Bring the w'end around again, coming under three cords and up and out of the last loop.

7 Finally, bring the w'end around and pass it through the centre of the knot, going over, under, under, over, under. Work the slack out very carefully, because if the knot is allowed to get out of shape, it will be almost impossible to correct.

CHINESE PLAFOND KNOT

A symmetrical but bulky ornamental lanyard knot.

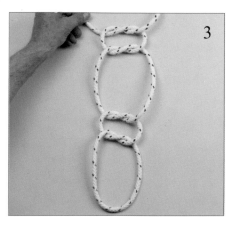

1 Middle the cord. Tie a half-knot, using both ends, and leaving a reasonable-sized bight in the end.

2 Tie an identical knot close to the first.

3 Tie two more identical half-knots a short distance from the first pair. This gives two slightly separated granny knots.

4 Invert the lower granny knot first, turning it from bottom to top.

5 Invert the upper granny knot and feed the bight up through the centre of the inverted granny.

6 The bight goes from the lower to the upper side, not through the centre hole.

7 This shows the passage of the bight through the granny knot.

8 Take the working end coming from the upper granny that naturally points towards you. Open up the lower granny.

9 Pass the w'end through the granny.

10 Take the other working end and pull it through the side loop.

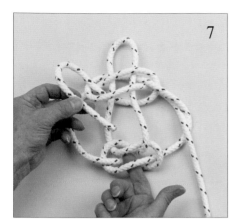

7

9

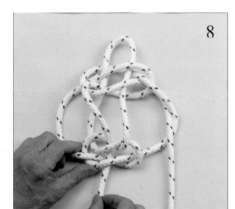

8

10

11

12

11 Pass the w'end down through the granny alongside the first w'end.

12 Make sure the top loop is long enough for its purpose, then carefully remove the slack, easing out towards the working ends. This is the most delicate part of the tying because improper tensioning and positioning of the parts will not give a good appearance.

BACK SPLICE

Instead of whipping the end of a rope to prevent unravelling, the ends of laid rope can be secured using a back splice. This will thicken the end of a rope so that it will not pass easily through a block without the risk of jamming.

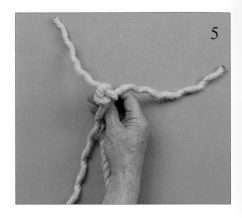

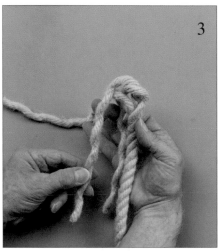

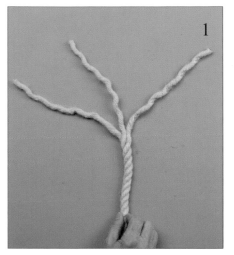

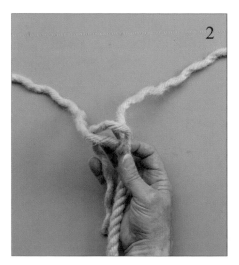

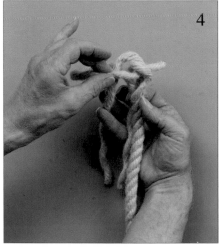

1 Unravel a few inches at the end of the rope. (It may help to put a constrictor around the rope to stop it unravelling more than is required.) Spread the strands out evenly.

2 Take one strand, and following the direction of the lay, fold it over the top of the rope and down between the other two strands. Leave a small gap at the top.

3 Do the same with one of the other strands. Fold over the first strand and lead it down beside the third strand.

4 The third strand now comes up over the second strand and tucks through the small gap left in Stage 1.

5 The result is a crown knot. The strands should be facing anti-clockwise at 120° intervals around the top of the rope.

6 Carefully ease the strands of the rope apart just below the crown to create a small gap.

7 Pass one of the strands from the crown over a strand of the rope and through the gap, i.e. beneath itself, and out of the rope again.

8 Repeat this for the other two strands from the crown, so that one strand is sticking out of each of the grooves between the main rope strands. Pull snug.

9 Continue to tuck over and under, working each strand in turn around the rope until three tucks have been completed (six for synthetic rope). Pull snug as each complete circuit of tucks is made. The excess ends may now be trimmed, but leave a bit sticking out which will gradually disappear with use.

10 Smooth the back splice in the traditional way by rolling it under your foot.

TIP It is easier to feed the strands through if you first wrap a piece of tape around the ends to contain any loose threads.

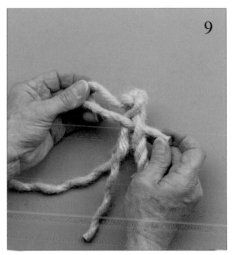

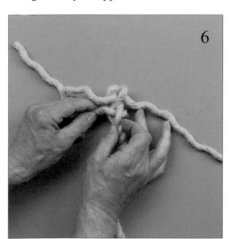

EYE SPLICE

This forms a permanent eye in the end of a rope and is stronger, if properly made, than a knotted eye. It may be 'soft', as in the photographs, or 'hard', when a metal or plastic thimble is inserted to reduce wear.

1 Unlay the rope for a few inches and apply a constrictor to prevent further unravelling. Tape the ends of the strands if required.

2 Bring the splayed end of the rope around to meet the main part to form an eye of the required size. Arrange it so that one strand lies on either side of the main rope, while the third strand lies along the rope. Separate the strands of the main rope. Feed one loose strand under the main strand closest to it, going against the lay.

234

3,4 Feed the second strand under the main strand next over from that under which the first strand passed.

5 Turn the eye over. Enter the third strand in the crack where the first strand emerged. Reverse its direction and bring it out of the only crack that is free. Each crack now has an eye strand emerging at the same level from it. Remove the constrictor and pull each strand, tensioning them evenly all round.

6 Continue to tuck one strand at a time (over 1/under1) against the lay, pulling firm when each round is complete. Make three complete tucks for natural fibre ropes but increase to six when splicing synthetics. Trim the ends but leave a little sticking out. This will disappear when tension is put on the eye.

5

6

CROW'S FOOT SPLICE

A crow's foot is raised when a rope is distorted in a certain fashion. This is quick and useful when a splice is needed in a hurry.

1

3

2

4

1 Decide where you want the eye. Grasp the rope firmly with both hands, just along the standing part from the chosen point.

2 Twist the rope in opposite directions while simultaneously pushing the hands together. The rope will distort and the strands will kink.

3 Continue to push the hands together to make the kinks stand up on their own stems. Work the kinks along the rope so that they are in line but separated by a strand from the next kink.

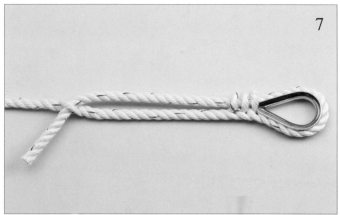

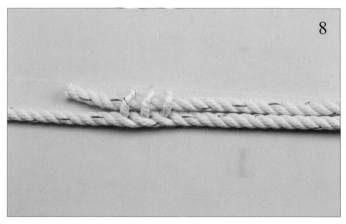

4 Open the loops of the kinks.

5 Feed the free end of the rope
  through the loops of the kinks in
sequence.

6 Insert a thimble into the eye with the
  point right up at the eye. Pull firmly
on the rope's end to hold it in place.

7 The end of the rope may then be
  passed between the strands of the
standing part to secure the splice OR

8 Make a further crow's foot a short
  way along the rope and pass the end
through the kink loops as before.
Loading on the eye will remove much of
the distortion and lock everything firm.

*CAUTION Once rope has had a crow's foot
inserted, it can never be restored to its original
condition.*

FOOTROPE KNOT

In the days of sail, the footrope stretched below the yards, and was all the sailors had to stand on when taking in a sail or working aloft.

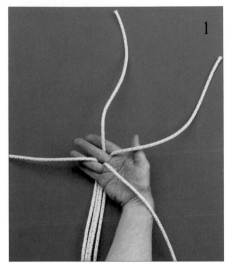

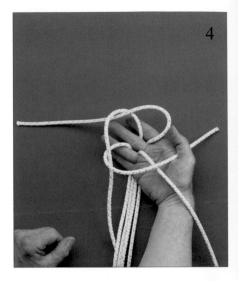

A footrope knot was worked on the footrope to give an extra foothold. It is shown here tied with four cords to gather them into one point.

1 Hold the four cords together and spread the working ends out at right angles.

2 Take any cord and fold it over the cord next to it, leaving a small eye.

3 Fold the cord that has just been crossed over the first cord and over the next cord.

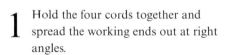

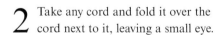

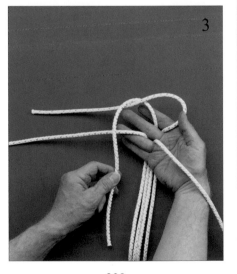

4 Take the third cord and fold it in the same fashion over cord two and over the fourth cord.

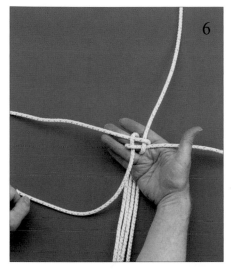

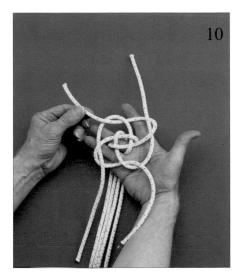

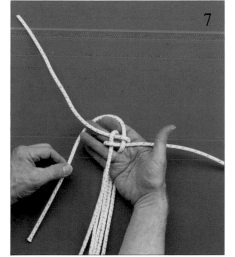

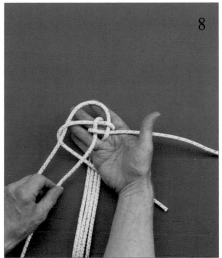

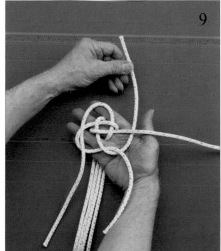

7 Now make a wall knot, which is the same as a crown knot but upside down. Take one cord and bring it under its neighbour, continuing in the same rotation as for the crown. Again, leave a small eye.

8 Pass the second cord under the one which has just crossed it and under its neighbour.

9 Repeat the previous step with the next cord.

10 Cross the fourth cord under the third cord and bring it out up through the small eye. This completes the wall knot.

CONTINUED OVERLEAF

5 Pass the fourth cord over the third, then feed it down through the small eye made by the first cord.

6 Pull out most of the slack but do not over-tighten. This is a crown knot with four strands made as we did when commencing a back splice.

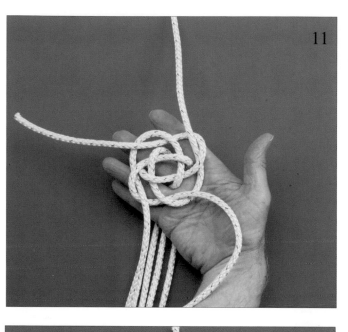

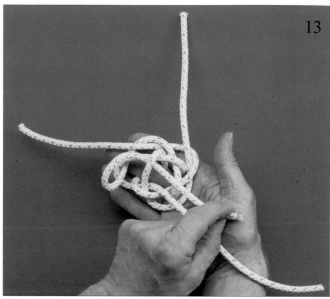

11 Work the knot up evenly, keeping the strands spread out. Having completed the crown knot and then the wall knot, we must get the ends to come out of the knot at the same place.

12, 13 Starting with any strand, tuck it up through the loop of the crown knot beside which it is lying. Repeat this last step for each of the other three cords.

14, 15 They do not cross any other strand but just come straight up through the appropriate crown loop.

16 Carefully and evenly work out the slack.

15

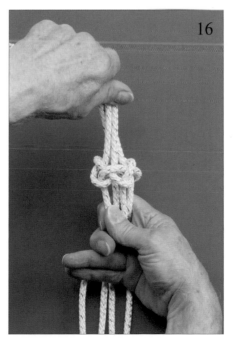
16

MATTHEW WALKER'S KNOT

This may be tied in any number of strands, from upwards of two, to make an attractive stopper knot. It is essential to maintain equal tension in the strands when manoeuvring the cords, so as to produce a pleasing and even appearance.

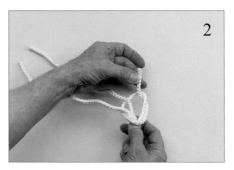

1 Unlay the strands to the point where the knot is to begin.

2 With one strand, go around behind all the other strands and come up in front to form a thumb knot.

3 Take the next strand around in front of the first strand.

4 Continue around behind the other strands, up through the loop of the first strand and then up in front of its own part, forming another thumb knot.

5 Bring the third strand around in front of the knot.

6 Follow around behind the other strands and up through both thumb knots and in front of its own part. This makes a third thumb knot.

7,8,9 Holding the ends near the top of the knot and the main cord just below, gently pull to tighten. The strands may need rearrangement or adjustment to get the correct sequence. This is best done before the final tightening.

Chapter Seven
CRAFTS

LEFT & BELOW: RAS TAFARI
The colours of the Ethiopian flag and the Rastafarian movement inspired this macramé wall hanging by Geoffrey Budworth.

OPPOSITE LEFT: DIAMONDS & DIAGONALS
Another wall hanging by Geoffrey Budworth. Tied with 52 strands of 3-mm diameter nylon cord, totalling 490 feet (150m) of line, it is embellished with glossy blue beads.

OPPOSITE RIGHT: RING TONES
Tied in 48 strands, with golden metal keyrings as extra ornamentation.

NOTE Macramé, or square knotting, consists merely of reef knots, half-knots and half hitches, all of which feature in this book, but which are artfully combined in their hundreds.

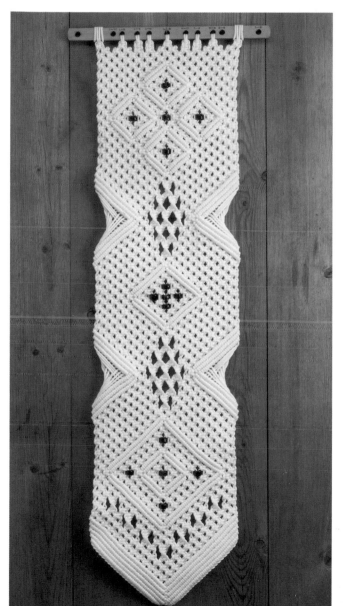

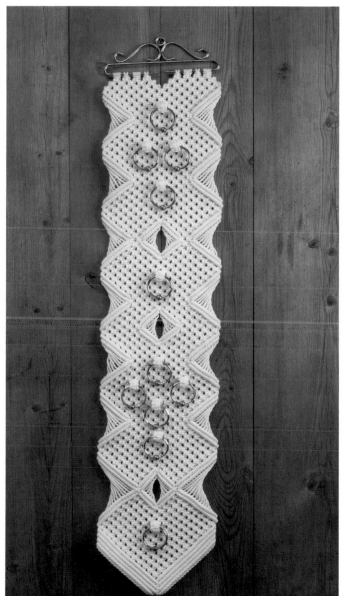

OPPOSITE: GYMNAST
A fanciful freestyle piece of Spanish hitching by Geoffrey Budworth.

ABOVE: SUBTLE SPHERE
Executed in steel and plastic wire by Ross Campbell of Fleetwood, Lancashire, U.K.

ABOVE CENTRE: CAT-OUT-OF-THE-BAG
An ornamental replica of a cat o'-nine-tails by professional ropeworker Des Pawson, of Ipswich, Suffolk, U.K.

ABOVE RIGHT: AMERICAN ATTIRE
A necktie from Seattle, U.S.A., utilizing twin Spanish ring knots and a sliding 5-lead x 4-bight Turk's head.

RIGHT: ANGLO-ALTERNATIVE
A necklet consisting of an eight-plait trefoil knot, tied in single strand by Geoffrey Budworth.

GLOSSARY

Abseil
This refers to a descent, controlled by the climber, on a rope which is often retrievable from the lower landing spot.

Anchorage
In boating, this is a general reference to mooring to the sea or river bed. In climbing, however, it is a safe belaying point or other secure attachment.

Belay
In rock-climbing terms, this is the process of attachment by rope and other fixings to an anchorage, while aboard a boat or ship it is to make fast to a cleat or pin.

Bend
A name given to any one of the knots that bind (or bend) two separate ropes together, so that they can be taken apart again.

Bight
The slack or bent portion of a rope or line between working end and standing end; also the curved rim part of a completed knot, such as a Turk's head.

Bight, In the
The process of tying a knot in the standing part of any cordage, without using either the working end or the standing end.

Breaking strength
A manufacturer's estimate of the load a rope will bear before it fails, expressed in kilograms and tonnes, taking no account of wear and tear, shock-loading, or knots that may reduce the figure drastically (see also Safe working load).

Cable
Strictly speaking, this is a thick rope created by three right-handed hawsers that have been laid up left-handed; but the term may also be loosely used to refer to any large-diameter rope.

Cord
A lashing, lanyard or other comparatively short length of line that is thinner than a rope.

Cordage
The collective term for rope, cord, twine and string.

Core
Fibres, yarns and monofilaments or multifilaments that either inertly fill the unwanted space within a rope construction, or that are a dynamic part of a rope covered in a braided sheath.

Crossing Point
Where one knot partly crosses another.

Draw-loop
The small loop left behind when the final tuck of a working end is not pulled completely through, so that the knot can be partially or wholly untied by simply tugging the w'end.

Dressing
This is the process of arranging any knot in its best possible layout before tightening it.

Efficiency
The actual strength of a knot, rope or smaller cord, expressed as a percentage of its theoretical breaking strength.

Fibre
The smallest element in cordage made from vegetable or animal material.

Frapping turn

One or more frapping turns are taken around a lashing or seizing, at right angles to the original turns, to tighten it.

Half hitch

A simple overhand or thumb knot, tied with the working end around its own adjacent standing part.

Halyard

A rope that is used to raise or lower a sail.

Hard-laid

Cordage that has considerable tension built in to it during manufacture, so that it is noticeably stiffer and harder to manipulate than that which is soft-laid.

Hawser

A three-stranded rope.

Hitch

Any knot used to belay a line and make it fast to an anchorage, such as a rail, spar, post, ring, tree trunk (suitably protected) or another rope.

Kernmantel

Construction used for climbing rope, consisting of a core contained within a tightly-woven protective sheath.

Kink

An over-tight loop in cordage, resulting in a damaging deformation.

Knot

The term for a stopper, loop and a self-sufficient binding, that excludes a bend or a hitch; it is also the generic term for all tucks and ties made in cordage.

Lanyard

A short length of cord used to lash, secure or suspend an object.

Lashing

A rope-binding that secures two or more poles or spars.

Lay

The direction in which each strand of a rope spirals, viewed as it recedes from the viewer's eye, either clockwise (right-handed or Z-laid) or counter-clockwise (left-handed or S-laid).

Lead (pronounced 'leed')

The path taken by the working end as it goes around or through an object or knot.

Line

Any rope with a specific function, for example, a towline, lifeline or washing line.

Locking tuck

The concluding lead of a working end that secures any knot in its finished state, without which it would unravel or collapse.

Loop

A bight with a crossing point. When it is formed by a w'end going over or on top of the initial lead, it is referred to as an overhand loop; when the w'end goes beneath, it is said to be an underhand loop. The word is also used to refer to any knot that forms a fixed, sliding or adjustable loop or loops.

Messenger

A throwing or heaving line, when it is used to haul a heavier rope across an intervening space (say from ship to quayside and vice versa) or to throw it up vertically.

Monofilament

Continuous synthetic thread of uniform circular cross-section, and of a diameter more than 1/500th inch (50 microns).

Multifilament

A bundle of very fine continuous synthetic threads of uniform circular cross-section and of a diameter less than 1/500th inch (50 microns).

GLOSSARY

Natural fibre
Processed products of plant and animal origin used to make cordage.

Nip
The location within any knot where friction may be concentrated.

Noose
A free-running, sliding or adjustable loop.

Polyamide
Commonly known as nylon, this was the first useful synthetic product that was made available to the cordage industry.

Polyester
A widely used synthetic cordage material (trade names: Dacron, Terylene).

Polyethylene
A polyolefin product commonly known as polythene/plastic.

Polypropylene
A versatile polyolefin product used by makers of cordage.

Racking turn
This is when a working end is taken in a figure of eight to make an extra-strong and stable lashing or seizing.

Rope
Cordage over 5/12th inch (10mm) in diameter.

Safe working load
The estimated load a rope can withstand, taking into account various weakening factors such as wear-and-tear, damage, effect of knots and usage, which may be as little as one-fifth or less of the rope's quoted breaking strength.

Security
The innate stability of a knot.

Shock cord
This is stretchy cordage made with a core of rubber strands and an extendable outer sheath.

S-laid
Left-handed, counter-clockwise.

Sling
A continuous length of rope, cord or webbing, also known as a strop.

Snugging
Only after a knot has been dressed should snugging be done, which is the process of removing unwanted slack prior to finally tightening the knot.

Soft-laid
The quality of rope or other cordage which is flexible and easy to manipulate.

Splice
A six-stranded plait executed in a three-stranded hawser-laid rope to form an eye or to prevent an end from unravelling.

Split film
Synthetic cordage made from a sheet of material reduced to ribbon-like filaments.

Stability
The degree to which any knot, bend or hitch will perform without distorting, capsizing and spilling.

Standing end
The inert end of any length of rope, cord or line not involved in the tying process. It is sometimes shortened to st'end or stend.

Standing part
That portion of cordage between the standing end and the working end.

Staple spun
The process of chopping a percentage of synthetic monofilaments into shorter staple lengths, so as to reproduce the

rough or hairy surface texture of natural fibre products.

Z-laid
Right-handed, clockwise.

Stopper
A knot tied in the end of any length of cordage to prevent it from fraying or pulling free from the main knot.

Strand
The largest element of a hawser, made from contra-twisted yarns.

Strength
The integral ability of knotted cordage to withstand a load.

Stuff
An informal term for cordage of all kinds.

Whipping
Any one of several tight bindings made with twine to prevent the cut end of cordage from fraying or unravelling.

Working end
The end (or ends) of any cordage involved in the tying process, sometimes referred to as a w'end or wend.

Yarn
The basic S-laid element of the strands of a rope made from natural fibre.

INDEX

FURTHER INFORMATION

THE MUSEUM OF KNOTS & SAILOR'S ROPEWORK

This unique collection of knotted artefacts, cordage and tools, both vintage and modern, has been accumulated by professional ropeworkers Des and Liz Pawson. It is a private, non-profit-making enterprise, housed at the bottom of their garden, and visitors come from the U.K., Europe and further afield to visit it. It celebrated its 10th anniversary in 2006. The museum is open by appointment throughout the year.

Contact Des and Liz: 501 Wherstead Road, Ipswich, Suffolk, IP2 8LL, U.K. Email: knots@footrope.fsnet.co.uk Telephone: +44 [0]1473 690 090)

THE INTERNATIONAL GUILD OF KNOT TYERS

Founded in 1982 by 25 individuals who met aboard the Royal Research Ship *Discovery* in St. Katharine's Dock, within sight of Tower Bridge), London, the IGKT is now a U.K.-registered charity committed to the study, practice and promotion of all aspects of knotting. It has a worldwide membership.

Members keep in touch via a quarterly magazine, *Knotting Matters,* which is a unique and useful forum of news, views and articles about knotting; while, for those able to travel to attend them, there are national, regional and local meetings, workshops, displays and demonstrations.

Membership is open to anyone interested in knots, whether accomplished professional, enthusiastic amateur dabbler or keen beginner. *To learn more, contact the IGKT. Honorary Secretary at: PO Box 3540, Chester, CH1 9FU, United Kingdom.*

Guild websites

IGKT

http://www.igkt.net/index.php

North Americas Branch

http://www.igktnab.org

Pacific Americas Branch

http://www.igktpab.org

Texas Branch

http://texasknot.tripod.com

RECORD-BREAKER

The *Guinness Book of Records* credits the fastest time for tying six Boy Scout knots to Clinton R. Bailey, Sr. of Pacific City, Oregon, U.S.A. The knots in question were the bowline; clove hitch; reef or square knot; round turn and two half hitches; sheepshank; and sheet bend. All of these knots feature in this book.

His time, achieved on 13 April 1977, when he was a 50-year-old disabled ex-naval veteran, remains an astonishing 8.1 seconds. This six-knot challenge has become a perennial crowd-puller at IGKT events but, despite many determined attempts, no one else has recorded a time lower than 12 seconds (with most aspiring record-breakers clocking around 16 seconds).

INTERNET SOURCES

Knotting thrives on the Internet and every aspect of interest, general or specialized, is represented. Simply key in 'knots' or 'knotting' and begin your search. Websites come and go, of course, but there are enough reliable links to lead you from basic knot-tying to a wide range of sites, including knots for arborists or tree surgeons, mathematical knots, computer-generated knots, knots for kite flyers, Celtic knotting, and the planting of herbaceous knot gardens.

Other websites

Knots on the Web, one of the widest-ranging links to knot-related sites covering all aspects of the subject. Compiled and run by Peter Suber. http://www.earlham.edu/~peters/knotlink.htm

Ropers Knot Page. This also has an amazing variety of links to knotting sites. The site is maintained by Ed Prins. http://www.realknots.com/knots/index.htm

These two sites will eventually provide the answers to your knotting questions and there are many other informative and helpful pages that will stimulate your interest and enthusiasm in the subject.

ACKNOWLEDGEMENTS

The illustrations of the knots in this book are by
Richard Jackson Photography.
Other photographs were supplied as follows: the Elizabethan Knot Garden
on page 13 is by courtesy of Hatfield House, Hertfordshire; and the
illustrations on pages 15, 16 and 17 were supplied by Nick Rains-PPL;
Peter Bentley/PPL and Bildagentur-online.com/Art Directors, respectively.
Almost all of the cordage used to illustrate this book was generously
provided by one or other of the following two U.K. suppliers:

English Braids, Spring Lane, Malvern, Worcestershire, WR14 1AL. The
company is one of Europe's foremost rope and cord manufacturers. It is
also a wholesale supplier with a diverse variety of products, ranging from
exhibition barrier ropes to webbing for lashing down road haulage loads;
but it specializes in quality cordage for the recreational marine market.
The marine sales division caters for the recreational sector and sail-boat
racing. To contact this company, telephone +44 (0)1684 892 222,
fax (0)1684 892 111, email www.englishbraids.com or key in website
www.englishbraids.com

Marlow Ropes Limited, Hailsham, East Sussex, BN27 3JS. Marlow has
for many years been a leading designer and manufacturer of cordage for
such specialized applications as aeronautics, civil engineering, climbing,
commercial shipping, the motor industry, oil exploration, utility and safety
work, mercantile and naval shipping and the army. It remains a market
leader in yacht rope technology and such accessories as shock cord, barrier
ropes, toe-strap and buoyancy bag webbing, whipping twines, splicing kits
and repair tapes. To contact this company, telephone +44 (0)1323 444 444,
fax (0)1323 444 456, or email info@marlowropes.com or see their website
http://www.marlowropes.com

BIBILIOGRAPHY

Asher, Dr. Harry, The Alternative Knot Book
Published London, 1989 by Nautical Books, an imprint of A. & C. Black Ltd. ISBN 0-7136-5950-5

Ashley, Clifford W., The Ashley Book of Knots
Revised edition 1993, first published in 1944 in New York by Doubleday, Doran & Company Inc., and in 1947 in London by Faber & Faber Ltd.

Grainger, Stuart, Creative Ropecraft
4th edition published London, 2000, by Adlard Coles Nautical, an imprint of A. & C. Black Ltd. ISBN 0-7136-5377-9

Griend, P. van de & Turner, J.C. (editors), The History & Science of Knots
Published Singapore, 1996 by World Scientific Publishing Co. Pte. Ltd. ISBN 981-02-2469-9

Hopkins, Richard, Knots
Published 2003 by Salamander Books Ltd. ISBN 1-84065-508-9

Miles, Roger E., Symmetric Bends – How to Join Two Lengths of Cord
Published Singapore, 1995 by World Scientific Publishing Co. Pte. Ltd. ISBN 981-02-2194-0

Pawson, Des, Knot Craft: 28 Ropework Projects
Published London, 2003 by Adlard Coles Nautical. ISBN 0-7-136-5441-4

Pennock, Skip, Decorative Woven Flat Knots
Published U.K., 2002 by the International Guild of Knot Tyers. ISBN 0-9515506-6-7

Rosenow, Frank, Seagoing Knots
Published New York, London, 1990 by W.W. Norton & Company. ISBN 0-393-03338-4

Shaw, John, The Directory of Knots
Published 2003 by Chartwell Books Inc. ISBN 0-7858-1629-1

Warner, Charles, A Fresh Approach to Knotting and Ropework
Published NSW, Australia, 1992 by the author. ISBN 0-9592036-3-X